COOKING ON CAMPUS

COOKING ON CAMPUS

PAVILION

First published in the United Kingdom in 2014 by
Pavilion
1 Gower Street
London
WC1E 6HD

The Good Housekeeping website is
www.goodhousekeeping.co.uk

10 9 8 7 6 5 4 3 2 1

ISBN 978-1-909397-94-1

A catalogue record for this book is available from
the British Library.

Reproduction by
Mission Productions Ltd, Hong Kong
Printed and bound by
1010 Printing International Ltd, China

This book can be ordered direct from the publisher
at www.pavilionbooks.com

NOTES

Both metric and imperial measures are given for
the recipes. Follow either set of measures, not a
mixture of both, as they are not interchangeable.

All spoon measures are level.
1 tsp = 5ml spoon; 1 tbsp = 15ml spoon.

Ovens and grills must be preheated to the specified
temperature.

Medium eggs should be used except where
otherwise specified. Free-range eggs are
recommended.

Note that some recipes contain raw or lightly
cooked eggs. The young, elderly, pregnant women
and anyone with an immune-deficiency disease
should avoid these because of the slight risk of
salmonella.

Contents

Breakfasts and Brunches

Stuff for the Kitchen

Although it's easiest to cook with a variety of utensils, it's amazing what you can get by without – but there are some essentials. There's no need to spend lots – cheaper shops have good selections that are fine for student days. If you can invest in a good cook's knife, however, it's worth the money. Look through the essentials list to see how many things are already in your kitchen and then stock up with the others.

ESSENTIALS

Pans
❑ Three saucepans with lids: small, medium and large
❑ Large frying pan
❑ Small frying pan

Measuring
❑ A 600ml (1 pint) measuring jug
❑ Measuring spoon

Draining, stirring and transferring
❑ A large sieve
❑ A large plastic spoon
❑ Wooden spoons

Bowls
❑ Two different-sized bowls

Cutting, chopping and peeling
❑ Three cook's knives: one large, one medium and a small serrated knife
❑ Bread knife
❑ Vegetable peeler
❑ Kitchen scissors
❑ Two chopping boards: one for vegetables or cooked food and one for raw meat, fish or poultry

Oven-cooking
❑ A roasting tin
❑ Ovenproof cooking dish
❑ Flameproof casserole

HANDY UTENSILS AND OTHER ITEMS

- ❑ Can opener
- ❑ Corkscrew
- ❑ Kettle
- ❑ Tea towels
- ❑ Toaster

USEFUL TO HAVE

- ❑ A kitchen scale

Stirring and transferring

- ❑ A whisk
- ❑ Rubber spatula (particularly if you like to bake)
- ❑ Tongs (handy for turning grilled foods and for serving spaghetti)
- ❑ Slotted spoon

Oven-cooking

- ❑ A baking tray

Handy utensils and other items

- ❑ A grater
- ❑ Potato masher
- ❑ Rolling pin

Electrical equipment

- ❑ Hand blender

Baking

- ❑ A large mixing bowl
- ❑ 20.5cm (8in) springform cake tin
- ❑ Wire rack
- ❑ Baking parchment

Baking without scales

As long as you have a tablespoon, you can measure out your baking ingredients without scales:

1 well-heaped tbsp flour = 25g (1oz)
1 rounded tbsp sugar = 25g (1oz)

Divide a block of butter in half to estimate 125g (4oz), half again for 50g (2oz), and again for 25g (1oz).

Energy-boosting Muesli

Hands-on time: 5 minutes

500g (1lb 2oz) porridge oats
100g (3½oz) toasted almonds, chopped
2 tbsp pumpkin seeds
2 tbsp sunflower seeds
100g (3½oz) ready-to-eat dried apricots, chopped
milk or yogurt to serve

1 Mix the oats with the almonds, seeds and apricots.
2 Store in a sealable container: it will keep for up to one month. Serve with milk or yogurt.

Makes 15 servings

Apple and Almond Yogurt

Hands-on time: 5 minutes, plus overnight chilling

500g (1lb 2oz) natural yogurt
50g (2oz) each sultanas and
    flaked almonds (see Savvy Swaps)
2 apples (see Savvy Swaps)

1 Put the yogurt into a bowl and add the sultanas and almonds.
2 Grate the apples, add to the bowl and mix together. Chill in the fridge overnight. Use as a topping for breakfast cereal or serve as a snack.

SAVVY SWAPS

· If you don't have any apples, you could use pears instead.
· You can also replace the sultanas with dried cranberries.

Serves 4

Porridge with Dried Fruit

Hands-on time: 5 minutes
Cooking time: 5 minutes

200g (7oz) porridge oats
400ml (14fl oz) milk, plus extra
  to serve
75g (3oz) mixture of chopped dried
  figs, apricots and raisins

1 Put the oats into a large pan and add the milk and 400ml (14fl oz) water. Stir in the figs, apricots and raisins and heat gently, stirring until the porridge thickens and the oats are cooked.
2 Divide among four bowls and serve with a splash of milk.

Serves 4

Perfect Pancakes

A stack of pancakes is the ultimate brunch-time treat! Whisk up a plateful with our simple step-by-step guide.

Making pancakes

To make 8 pancakes, you will need:

125g (4oz) plain flour
a pinch of salt
1 medium egg
300ml (½ pint) milk
oil or butter to fry

1. Sift the flour and salt into a bowl, make a well in the middle and whisk in the egg. Work in the milk, then leave to stand for 20 minutes.
2. Heat a pan and coat lightly with oil or butter. Pour just a little batter into the pan and swirl to coat the bottom of the pan.

3 Cook for 1½–2 minutes until golden, carefully turning once. Remove from the pan on to a warmed plate, and repeat with the remaining batter.

Savoury pancake fillings

Almost any mixture of cooked vegetables, fish or chicken, flavoured with herbs and moistened with a little soured cream or cream cheese can be used. Try the following – just spoon on to the pancake, fold over and serve:

1 Mix 25g (1oz) each grated cheese and chopped ham with 1 tbsp crème fraîche (or use mayonnaise).
2 Cooked mixed vegetables.
3 Sautéed spinach, pinenuts and feta cheese.
4 Smoked fish such as haddock and chopped hard-boiled egg with soured cream.

3

SAVVY SWAP

Use half milk and half water if you don't have enough milk.

Lemon and Blueberry Pancakes

Hands-on time: 15 minutes
Cooking time: about 15 minutes

125g (4oz) wholemeal plain flour
1 tsp baking powder
¼ tsp bicarbonate of soda
2 tbsp golden caster sugar
finely grated zest of 1 lemon
125g (4oz) natural yogurt
2 tbsp milk
2 medium eggs
40g (1½oz) butter
100g (3½oz) blueberries (see Savvy Swap)
1 tsp sunflower oil
natural yogurt and fruit compôte to serve

1 Sift the flour, baking powder and bicarbonate of soda into a bowl. Add the sugar and lemon zest. Pour in the yogurt and milk. Break the eggs into the mixture and whisk together.

2 Melt 25g (1oz) butter in a pan, add to the bowl with the blueberries and stir everything together.

3 Heat a dot of butter with the oil in a frying pan over a medium heat until hot. Add four large spoonfuls of the mixture to the pan to make four pancakes. After about 2 minutes, flip them over and cook for 1–2 minutes. Repeat with the remaining mixture, adding a dot more butter each time.

4 Serve with natural yogurt and some fruit compôte.

SAVVY SWAP

Instead of fresh blueberries and lemon, use 100g (3½oz) chopped ready-to-eat dried apricots and 2 tsp grated fresh root ginger.

18

Serves 4

Pancakes with Bacon and Syrup

Hands-on time: 20 minutes
Cooking time: about 20 minutes

300g (11oz) self-raising flour
1 tsp baking powder
25g (1oz) caster sugar
2 large eggs
75g (3oz) natural yogurt
300ml (½ pint) semi-skimmed milk
40g (1½oz) butter
12 unsmoked streaky bacon rashers
25g (1oz) maple syrup
75g (3oz) golden syrup

1 Preheat the oven to 110°C (90°C fan oven) mark ¼ (for warming). Sift the flour, baking powder and sugar into a large bowl and stir to combine. In a large jug, whisk the eggs, yogurt and milk together until smooth. Using a whisk, gently stir the wet ingredients into the dry ones until just combined (the mixture may be a little lumpy, but don't worry).

2 Heat a knob of the butter in a large frying pan until foaming, then drop large serving spoonfuls of the batter into the pan, spacing them apart (cook in batches). Cook the pancakes for 2–3 minutes until the underside is golden and the tops look dry and bubbly, then flip and cook for another 2–3 minutes until golden. Put the cooked pancakes on a baking tray, cover with foil and keep warm in the oven. Repeat with the remaining batter.

3 Meanwhile, fry the bacon in a large, non-stick frying pan until it is crisp and golden.

4 In a small jug or serving bowl, stir together the maple and golden syrups. Serve the warm pancakes stacked with the bacon, drizzled with the syrup.

Serves 4

Good Eggs

There are numerous ways to cook with eggs using simple techniques such as frying, poaching and scrambling. Follow these instructions for perfect results.

How to fry an egg

1 Break an egg into a bowl or cup, so that if any shell falls in you can scoop it out with a teaspoon.
2 Heat 1 tbsp vegetable or sunflower oil in a non-stick frying pan for 1 minute. If you don't have a non-stick pan use 3 tbsp oil.
3 Turn the heat down low and carefully pour the egg into the hot fat. (If the heat is too high, the white will burn before the yolk is cooked.)
4 Tilt the pan and use a large spoon to scoop the fat up and pour it over the yolk.
5 Cook until the yolk is just set.

How to poach an egg

1 Fill a deep frying pan two-thirds full with water and bring to the boil.
2 Break an egg on to a saucer and slide carefully into the water.
3 Using a large metal spoon, gently roll the egg over two or three times to wrap the white around the yolk. Take the pan off the heat, cover and leave to stand for 3 minutes. Serve immediately. Use a slotted spoon to remove the egg from the pan.

How to scramble eggs

1 Lightly beat 2 medium eggs in a bowl with a fork. Season with salt and ground black pepper.
2 Melt a knob of butter in a small pan over a low heat and pour in the eggs.
3 Start stirring immediately, to break up the lumps as they form and keep the eggs moving while cooking. When they are the consistency you prefer – soft or firmer – remove from the heat.

How to boil an egg

Bring a small pan of water to the boil. Once the water is boiling, add a medium egg. For a soft-boiled egg, cook for 6 minutes and for hard-boiled, cook for 10 minutes. Using a slotted spoon, remove the egg from the hot water and serve.

How to bake eggs

1 Preheat the oven – see step 3. Generously smear individual baking dishes or one large baking dish with butter.

2 Put in any accompaniments, if using (see Cook's Trick). If using a vegetable-based accompaniment, use the back of a spoon to make a hollow or hollows in it in which to break the egg or eggs. Carefully break the egg or eggs into the hollows.

3 Bake for 8–10 minutes at 200°C (180°C fan oven) mark 6, or 15–18 minutes at 180°C (160°C fan oven) mark 4, until the whites are just set; the yolks should still be quite runny.

3

2

COOK'S TRICK

· Eggs are delicious baked on top of well-cooked vegetables. Try spinach or lightly fried potatoes.

How to make an omelette

There are numerous different types of omelette – from the folded omelette made from simple beaten eggs to thick omelettes such as Spanish tortilla and Italian frittata.

To serve 1, you will need:
15g (½oz) butter
2 medium eggs, beaten and
    seasoned with salt and pepper

1 Add the butter to a preheated small frying pan and let it sizzle for a few moments without browning, then pour in the beaten, seasoned eggs and stir a few times with a fork.
2 As the omelette begins to stick at the sides of the pan, lift it up and let the uncooked egg run into the gap.
3 When the omelette is nearly set and the underneath is brown, loosen the edges and give the pan a sharp shake to slide the omelette across.
4 Add a filling (such as grated cheese or fried mushrooms) if you like, and fold the far side of the omelette towards you. Tilt the pan to slide the omelette on to the plate and serve.

1

3

Spanish Omelette

Hands-on time: 15 minutes
Cooking time: about 45 minutes

900g (2lb) potatoes, peeled and
  left whole
3–4 tbsp vegetable oil
1 onion, finely sliced
8 medium eggs
3 tbsp freshly chopped flat-leafed
  parsley
3 streaky bacon rashers
salt and freshly ground black pepper
green salad to serve

1 Add the potatoes to a pan of lightly
  salted water, bring to the boil,
  reduce the heat and simmer for
  15–20 minutes until almost cooked.
  Drain and leave until cool enough to
  handle, then slice thickly.
2 Heat 1 tbsp oil in an 18cm (7in)
  non-stick frying pan (suitable for
  use under the grill). Add the onion
  and fry gently for 7–10 minutes until
  softened. Take the pan off the heat
  and put to one side.
3 Lightly beat the eggs in a bowl and
  season well.

4 Preheat the grill. Heat the remaining
  oil in the frying pan, then layer
  the potato slices, onion and 2 tbsp
  chopped parsley in the pan. Pour in
  the beaten eggs and cook for 5–10
  minutes until the omelette is firm
  underneath. Meanwhile, grill the
  bacon until golden and crisp, and
  then break into pieces.
5 Put the omelette in the pan under
  the grill for 2–3 minutes until the top
  is just set. Sprinkle the bacon and
  remaining chopped parsley over the
  surface. Serve cut into wedges, with
  a green salad.

Serves 4

Huevos Rancheros

Hands-on time: 10 minutes
Cooking time: about 15 minutes

1 tbsp vegetable oil

1 medium red onion, finely sliced

1 each yellow and red pepper, seeded
  and finely sliced

1 red chilli, seeded and finely sliced
  (see Safety Tip)

2 × 400g cans chopped tomatoes

½ tsp dried mixed herbs

4 large eggs

a small handful of fresh flat-leafed
  parsley, roughly chopped (optional)

crusty bread to serve

SAFETY TIP

Chillies can be quite mild to
blisteringly hot, depending on the
type of chilli and its ripeness. Taste
a small piece first to check it's not
too hot for you. Be extremely careful
when handling chillies not to touch
or rub your eyes with your fingers,
or they will sting. Wash knives
immediately after handling chillies.
As a precaution, use rubber gloves
when preparing them, if you like.

1 Heat the oil in a large frying pan
  over a high heat. Fry the onion,
  peppers and chilli for 3 minutes
  until just softened. Add the
  tomatoes and dried herbs. Season
  and simmer for 3 minutes.

2 Break an egg into a small cup. Use
  a wooden spoon to scrape a hole in
  the tomato mixture, then quickly
  drop in the egg. Repeat with the
  remaining eggs, spacing evenly
  around the tomato mixture. Cover
  and simmer for 3–5 minutes until
  the eggs are just set. Sprinkle with
  parsley if you like, and serve with
  crusty bread.

Serves 6

Sunday Brunch Bake

Hands-on time: 15 minutes
Cooking time: about 35 minutes

butter to grease
6 English muffins
1½–2 tbsp wholegrain mustard
6 streaky bacon rashers
12 raw cocktail sausages
600ml (1 pint) semi-skimmed milk
4 large eggs
2 tbsp chives, freshly chopped, plus
   extra to garnish (optional)
40g (1½oz) mature Cheddar, grated
a large handful of cherry tomatoes
salt and freshly ground black pepper
baked beans to serve (optional)

1 Preheat the oven to 200°C
  (180°C fan oven) mark 6. Grease
  an ovenproof rectangular dish
  roughly 22 × 33cm (8½ × 13in)
  and put to one side.

2 Split the muffins in half horizontally
  and spread the cut sides with
  mustard. Next, cut each bacon
  rasher in half to make two shorter
  pieces. Arrange the muffins, cut side
  up, and bacon in the dish, then dot
  around the sausages.

3 In a large jug, mix together the
  milk, eggs, chives, if you like, and
  some seasoning. Pour the mixture
  over the muffins, then sprinkle the
  grated cheese and cherry tomatoes
  over the top.

4 Bake for 30–35 minutes until the
  sausages are golden and the liquid
  has set. Garnish with chives, if
  using, and serve immediately
  with baked beans, if you like.

Serves 6

All-day Breakfast Burger

Hands-on time: 30 minutes
Cooking time: 25 minutes

1 tbsp olive oil
150g (5oz) mushrooms, finely chopped
½ small onion, finely chopped
2 tbsp tomato ketchup
1 tbsp Worcestershire sauce
500g (1lb 2oz) pork mince
3 tbsp flat-leafed parsley,
   freshly chopped
8 streaky bacon rashers
4 medium eggs
salt and freshly ground black pepper
2 English muffins, halved and toasted,
   to serve

1 Heat the oil over a high heat in a large, non-stick frying pan and cook the mushrooms for 5 minutes or until tender. Empty into a large bowl and put the pan to one side.

2 Add the onion, tomato ketchup, Worcestershire sauce, pork mince, parsley and plenty of seasoning to the bowl and mix to combine.

3 Divide the mixture equally into four and shape each portion into a flattened patty.

4 Put the pan back on to a medium heat and fry the burgers for 15–18 minutes, turning occasionally, until cooked through.

5 Meanwhile, heat another frying pan and cook the bacon rashers until golden and crisp. Drain on kitchen paper. Crack the eggs into the empty pan and fry them over a gentle heat until the whites are set and the yolks are still soft.

6 Serve each burger on half a toasted muffin, topped with some bacon and a fried egg. Season to taste.

Serves 4

In for Lunch

Take 5 Steps to Healthy Eating

It's easy to make delicious food that is healthy – even when you're cooking on a budget. In fact, some of the healthiest foods are really cheap – take pulses, for example. Canned chickpeas can be whizzed up to make hummus or added to a tomato sauce or curry and served with pasta or rice for one of the healthiest meals you could find. Canned fish and cheaper cuts of chicken, such as thighs, make tasty, nourishing meals. Here are our top 5 steps to healthy eating.

1 As a rough guide, fill about half your plate with plenty of vegetables as a good way of getting your 'five a day'. Always choose a variety, to get a wide range of nutrients. An easy way is to have a leafy green, plus something red or yellow at least. Your protein portion will then take about a quarter of the plate and your rice or potatoes the other quarter. If you have a pasta dish you might like to eat it with a side salad.

2 Always have a small amount of protein: meat, fish, eggs, beans, tofu, Quorn, seeds or nuts. Even if you're not a vegetarian, have some vegetarian meals in a week. They are cheap and tasty as well as nutritious.

3 Eggs, oily fish, unsalted nuts and seeds contain 'essential' fats that your body needs for good health, so eat these regularly every week.

4   Dairy foods can make simple and tasty meals. A cheese sauce goes well with vegetables or pasta, or yogurt takes the heat out of a curry. Be careful of adding cheese to too many meals, though, as you can have too much saturated fat this way. Saturated fat is found in dairy foods and meat and has been linked to ill health and obesity, so it's wise to keep portions of cheese small and have just a light spreading of butter. Go for leaner cuts of meat or trim off the fat, if possible.

5   Choose wholegrain varieties of starchy foods like bread, rice and pasta whenever you can.

Quick Winter Minestrone

Hands-on time: 10 minutes
Cooking time: 45 minutes

2 tbsp olive oil

1 small onion, finely chopped

1 carrot, chopped

1 celery stick, chopped

1 garlic clove, crushed

2 tbsp freshly chopped thyme

1 litre (1¾ pints) hot vegetable stock (see Take Stock)

400g can chopped tomatoes

400g can borlotti beans, drained and rinsed

125g (4oz) minestrone pasta (see Savvy Swap)

175g (6oz) Savoy cabbage, shredded

salt and freshly ground black pepper

pesto to serve

toasted ciabatta drizzled with extra virgin olive oil to serve (optional)

1 Heat the oil in a large pan and add the onion, carrot and celery. Cook for 8–10 minutes until softened, then add the garlic and thyme and fry for another 2–3 minutes.

2 Add the hot stock, tomatoes and half the borlotti beans. Mash the remaining beans, stir into the soup and simmer for 30 minutes, adding the minestrone pasta and cabbage for the last 10 minutes of cooking time.

3 Check the seasoning, then serve in individual bowls with a dollop of pesto on top and slices of toasted ciabatta drizzled with extra virgin olive oil, if you like, on the side.

TAKE STOCK

You can use 2 vegetable stock cubes dissolved in 1 litre (1¾ pints) boiling water.

SAVVY SWAP

Instead of minestrone pasta you can use small pasta shapes or spaghetti snapped into lengths.

38

Sweetcorn Soup with Quesadilla Wedges

Hands-on time: 15 minutes
Cooking time: about 25 minutes

1.3 litres (2¼ pints) chicken stock
100ml (3½fl oz) semi-skimmed milk
1kg bag frozen sweetcorn
1 medium potato, roughly chopped
1 cooked skinless chicken breast,
   finely chopped
½ avocado, finely chopped
40g (1½oz) mature Cheddar,
   finely grated
few dashes Tabasco sauce, to taste
a small handful of fresh coriander,
   chopped, plus extra to garnish
2 flour tortilla wraps
salt and freshly ground black pepper

1 Put the stock and milk into a large pan and add the sweetcorn and potato. Bring to the boil, then reduce the heat and simmer for 15 minutes or until the potato is cooked.

2 Meanwhile, put the chicken, avocado, cheese, Tabasco and coriander into a bowl with plenty of seasoning and stir to combine.

3 Blend the soup with a hand blender until very smooth (do this in batches, if necessary). Pour the soup back into the pan. Check the seasoning.

4 Heat a griddle pan over a medium heat, then lay a tortilla in the pan. Spoon the chicken mixture over the tortilla, then press on a second tortilla. Heat for 3–5 minutes, then flip it (slide on to a plate, then put another plate on top, invert it, then slide it back into the pan) and cook for another 3–5 minutes.

5 Meanwhile, reheat the soup. Ladle into bowls and garnish with coriander. Cut the quesadilla into wedges and serve with the soup.

SAVVY SWAP

Instead of frozen sweetcorn, use the equivalent amount of tinned.

40

Serves 4

Mexican Corn Wraps

Hands-on time: 20 minutes

410g can kidney beans, drained and rinsed

50g (2oz) soured cream

juice of ½ lemon

1 cob sweetcorn

¼–½ red onion, to taste, finely chopped

125g (4oz) cherry tomatoes, halved

2 tbsp tomato ketchup

½–1 tsp chipotle paste

a large handful of fresh coriander leaves, roughly chopped

4 large flour tortilla wraps

¼ iceberg lettuce, shredded

75g (3oz) mature Cheddar, grated

salt and freshly ground black pepper

1 Whiz the beans, soured cream, lemon juice and plenty of seasoning with a hand blender until smooth. Put to one side.

2 Put the sweetcorn on its end on a board and use a sharp knife to slice the kernels off the cob, working from the top to the bottom. Discard the cob and put the kernels into a large bowl with the red onion, cherry tomatoes, ketchup, chipotle paste and coriander. Stir to combine and check the seasoning.

3 Put a tortilla on a board and smear a quarter of the bean purée in a line along the centre, leaving a 5cm (2in) border at each end. Top with a quarter each of the lettuce, sweetcorn mixture and Cheddar. Fold the sides of the tortilla over the filling, then roll up to enclose (secure in place with a cocktail stick if you like). Slice the wraps in half and serve.

Chicken Club Sandwich

Hands-on time: 20 minutes

12 slices good-quality white bread, freshly toasted

4 tsp wholegrain mustard

3 tomatoes, thinly sliced

40g (1½oz) mature Cheddar, grated

a large handful of fresh basil leaves

4 tsp mayonnaise

2 cooked skinless chicken breasts, sliced, about 200g (7oz)

1 large avocado, peeled, stoned and thinly sliced

a large handful of rocket

salt and freshly ground black pepper

chips to serve (optional)

1 Lay four slices toasted bread on a board. Spread each with 1 tsp mustard, then divide the tomato slices, cheese and basil equally among the four slices. Press another slice of toast on to each stack.

2 Spread the top toast of each stack with 1 tsp mayonnaise, then divide the chicken, avocado and rocket equally among the stacks. Season, then press the final slice of toast on to each stack.

3 Cut the stacks into quarters diagonally, then secure each quarter with a cocktail stick. Serve immediately with chips, if you like.

Serves 4

Snazzy Cheese on Toast

Hands-on time: 5 minutes
Cooking time: 5 minutes

2 thick slices bread
2 tbsp cranberry sauce
75g (3oz) blue cheese (Stilton is good)

1 Preheat the grill. Toast the bread lightly on both sides.

2 Spread one side of each with 1 tbsp cranberry sauce.

3 Crumble the cheese and sprinkle on top of the cranberry sauce.

4 Put each slice under the hot grill until the cheese melts, then eat the toast immediately.

Warm Lentil and Egg Salad

Hands-on time: 15 minutes
Cooking time: about 40 minutes

1 tbsp olive oil

1 onion, 1 carrot and 1 celery stick, finely chopped

2 red peppers, seeded and roughly chopped

200g (7oz) closed cup mushrooms, sliced

200g (7oz) brown lentils, rinsed and drained

600ml (1 pint) hot vegetable stock (see Take Stock)

4 medium eggs

100g (3½oz) baby spinach leaves or shredded spinach leaves

2 tbsp balsamic vinegar

freshly ground black pepper

1 Heat the oil in a large pan. Add the onion, carrot and celery and cook for 5 minutes. Add the peppers and mushrooms. Cover and cook for another 5 minutes. Stir in the lentils and hot stock. Bring to the boil, reduce the heat, cover and simmer for 25–30 minutes.

2 Meanwhile, bring a large pan of water to the boil. Break the eggs into the water and cook for 3–4 minutes. Lift the poached eggs out with a slotted spoon, drain on kitchen paper and keep warm.

3 A couple of minutes before the end of the lentil cooking time, add the spinach and cook until wilted. Stir in the vinegar. Spoon on to four plates or bowls and top each with a poached egg. Season with ground black pepper and serve.

TAKE STOCK

You can use 1 vegetable stock cube dissolved in 600ml (1 pint) boiling water.

Potato Salad

Hands-on time: 10 minutes
Cooking time: about 20 minutes, plus cooling

550g (1¼lb) new potatoes
6 tbsp mayonnaise
2 tbsp crème fraîche
  (see Savvy Swaps)
2 tbsp white wine vinegar
2 shallots, finely chopped
  (see Savvy Swaps)
4 tbsp chopped gherkins (optional)
2 tbsp olive oil
salt and freshly ground black pepper

1 Cook the potatoes in a pan of lightly salted boiling water for 15–20 minutes until tender. Drain, leave to cool slightly, then chop.

2 Mix together the mayonnaise, crème fraîche, vinegar, shallots, gherkins, if you like, and oil. Season with salt and ground black pepper and mix with the potatoes. Leave to cool, then chill until ready to serve.

SAVVY SWAPS

• Use 8 tbsp mayonnaise instead of crème fraîche.
• Use spring onions instead of shallots.

Serves 4

Spicy Beans with Potatoes

Hands-on time: 12 minutes
Cooking time: about 1½ hours

4 baking potatoes
1 tbsp olive oil, plus extra to rub
1 tsp smoked paprika, plus a pinch
1 small onion, finely chopped
1 tbsp freshly chopped rosemary
400g can cannellini beans, drained
  and rinsed
400g can chopped tomatoes
1 tbsp light brown sugar
1 tsp Worcestershire sauce
75ml (2½fl oz) red wine
75ml (2½fl oz) hot vegetable stock
a small handful of freshly chopped
  flat-leafed parsley (optional)
grated mature Cheddar to sprinkle
sea salt and freshly ground
  black pepper

1 Preheat the oven to 200°C (180°C fan oven) mark 6. Rub the potatoes with a little oil and put them on a baking tray. Sprinkle with sea salt and a pinch of smoked paprika and bake for 1–1½ hours.

2 Meanwhile, heat the 1 tbsp oil in a large pan, then fry the shallots over a low heat for 1–2 minutes until they start to soften.

3 Add the rosemary and the 1 tsp paprika and fry for 1–2 minutes, then add the beans, tomatoes, sugar, Worcestershire sauce, wine and hot stock. Season, then bring to the boil, reduce the heat and simmer, uncovered, for 10–15 minutes. Serve with the baked potatoes, sprinkled with parsley, if you like, and grated Cheddar.

SAVVY SWAP

For a quick meal that takes less than 25 minutes, the spicy beans are just as good served with toast.

Serves 4

Pasta Days

Perfect Pasta

How to cook dried pasta

1 Fill a big pan with plenty of water. Cover and bring to the boil, then once it's boiling keep the heat high so that it's constantly boiling. This will stop the pasta sticking together. Add 1 tsp salt to the water.

2 Allow 125g (4oz) pasta per person. Tip the pasta into the boiling water and stir once. If you're using spaghetti, push it into the pan and, as the ends soften, coil them round in the pan to immerse all the spaghetti in the water. Set the timer for 1 minute less than the time stated on the pack and cook uncovered.

3 Check the pasta when the timer goes off. It should be cooked al dente: tender with a little bite at the centre. If it's done drain well. Otherwise, cook for another 30 seconds and taste again. Drain in a colander.

How to cook fresh pasta

Fresh pasta is cooked in the same way as dried, but for a shorter time.

1 Bring the water to the boil. Add the pasta to the boiling water all at once and stir well.
2 Set the timer for 2 minutes and keep testing every 30 seconds until the pasta is cooked al dente: tender, but with a bite at the centre. Drain in a colander.

COOK'S TRICK

Don't be distracted from draining the pasta as soon as it's ready. If you leave it in the water for too long, it will turn soggy and can't be rescued. If you're not ready to serve the pasta right away, drain, return it to the pan and add a drizzle of oil to stop it sticking. The cooked pasta will be OK covered for 5–10 minutes.

All-round Tomato Sauce

Use this as a base for pastas, pizzas and meaty sauces. It will keep in the fridge for up to a week in an airtight, non-metallic container.

Hands-on time: 15 minutes
Cooking time: about 25 minutes
Serves 4

1 glug olive oil
1 medium onion, roughly chopped
1 garlic clove, peeled and chopped
2 × 400g cans chopped tomatoes
2 tbsp tomato ketchup
1 tbsp dried mixed herbs
salt and freshly ground
black pepper

1 Heat the oil in a large pan over a low heat, then add the onion and fry, stirring occasionally, for 10 minutes or until translucent.
2 Stir in the other ingredients and some seasoning, then bring to the boil. When bubbling, reduce the heat to low and continue to cook for 15 minutes, stirring occasionally until thick and pulpy. Your sauce is now ready to use.

Six super student sauce recipes

White Sauce

Put 50g (2oz) butter, 50g (2oz) plain flour and 568ml carton milk in a microwaveable bowl. Use a balloon whisk to whisk together, then microwave on full power in an 800W microwave for 5 minutes, whisking every 1 minute, until smooth and thickened. Season with grated nutmeg, salt and ground black pepper.

Tomato, Prawn and Garlic Pasta Sauce

Put 350g (12oz) cooked peeled prawns into a bowl with 4 tbsp tomato purée and stir well. Heat 1 tbsp olive oil and 15g (½oz) butter in a frying pan and gently cook 3 peeled and sliced garlic cloves until golden. Add 4 large chopped tomatoes and 125ml (4fl oz) dry white wine. Leave the sauce to bubble for about 5 minutes, then stir in the prawns and some freshly chopped parsley.

COOK'S TRICK

Add the milk to the white sauce gradually and stir thoroughly after each addition. If the sauce is lumpy, simply push it through a sieve.

Courgette and Anchovy Pasta Sauce

Heat the oil from a 50g can anchovies in a frying pan. Add 1 peeled and crushed garlic clove and a pinch of dried chilli and cook for 1 minute. Add 400ml (14fl oz) passata sauce (puréed and sieved tomatoes, available in jars), 2 diced courgettes and the anchovies. Bring to the boil, then reduce the heat and simmer for about 10 minutes, stirring well, until the anchovies have melted.

Mushrooms and Cream Pasta Sauce

Heat 1 tbsp olive oil in a large pan and fry 1 finely chopped onion for 7–10 minutes until soft. Add 300g (11oz) sliced mushrooms and cook for 3–4 minutes. Pour in 125ml (4fl oz) dry white wine and bubble for 1 minute, then stir in 500ml (18fl oz) low-fat crème fraîche. Heat until bubbling, then stir in 2 tbsp freshly chopped tarragon. Season with salt and ground black pepper.

Lemon and Parmesan Pasta Sauce

Cook pasta shells in a large pan of lightly salted boiling water for the time stated on the pack. Add 125g (4oz) frozen peas to the pasta water for the last 5 minutes of the cooking time. Drain the pasta and peas, put back into the pan and add the grated zest and juice of ½ a lemon and 75g (3oz) freshly grated Parmesan. Season with ground black pepper, toss and serve immediately.

Broccoli and Thyme Pasta Sauce

Put 900g (2lb) trimmed broccoli into a pan with 150ml (¼ pint) hot vegetable stock. Bring to the boil, then cover, reduce the heat and simmer for 3–4 minutes until tender – the stock should have evaporated. Add 2 peeled and crushed garlic cloves and 2 tbsp olive oil and cook for 1–2 minutes to soften the garlic. Add 250g carton mascarpone, 2 tbsp freshly chopped thyme and 100g (3½oz) freshly grated cheese and mix together. Season to taste.

Simple Chilli Pasta

Hands-on time: 5 minutes
Cooking time: about 12 minutes

350g (12oz) spaghetti

1 tbsp olive oil

2 garlic cloves, crushed

1 red chilli, seeded and chopped
  (see Safety Tip, page 28)

2 × 400g cans chopped tomatoes
  with herbs

20g pack fresh basil

50g (2oz) pitted black olives

salt

1 Cook the spaghetti in a large pan of lightly salted boiling water for the time stated on the pack. Drain and put back into the pan.

2 Meanwhile, heat the oil in another pan. Tip the garlic and chilli into the pan and fry for 2 minutes, stirring all the time. Add the tomatoes and cook for 5 minutes or until bubbling.

3 Tear the basil leaves and add them to the tomatoes with the olives. Tip the mixture into the drained spaghetti, stir well and serve.

Serves 4

Quick Carbonara

Hands-on time: 10 minutes
Cooking time: about 15 minutes

350g (12oz) linguine or spaghetti
½ tbsp olive oil
200g (7oz) bacon lardons
4 large eggs, beaten
75g (3oz) freshly grated Parmesan,
  plus extra to garnish
salt and freshly ground black pepper
a small handful of fresh parsley,
  chopped, to garnish (optional)

1 Bring a large pan of water to the boil and cook the linguine for the time stated on the pack until it is al dente.
2 Meanwhile, heat the oil in a large frying pan and fry the bacon lardons for 5 minutes or until golden. Take the pan off the heat.
3 In a medium bowl, mix together the eggs, grated Parmesan and plenty of ground black pepper.
4 Drain the pasta, keeping 100ml (3½fl oz) of the cooking water to one side. Put the bacon pan back on to a low heat and stir in the pasta water, pasta and egg mixture. Stir for 1 minute or until thickened. Check the seasoning, garnish with the parsley, if you like, and extra Parmesan and serve.

Serves 4

Chicken, Bacon and Leek Pasta Bake

Hands-on time: 10 minutes
Cooking time: about 20 minutes

1 tbsp olive oil

100g (3½oz) chopped streaky bacon rashers

450g (1lb) boneless, skinless chicken thighs, chopped

3 medium leeks, chopped

300g (11oz) macaroni or other pasta shapes

350g carton ready-made cheese sauce

2 tsp Dijon mustard

2 tbsp freshly chopped flat-leafed parsley

25g (1oz) freshly grated Parmesan

salt

1. Heat the oil in a large frying pan. Add the bacon and chicken and cook for 7–8 minutes. Add the leeks and continue cooking for 4–5 minutes.

2. Meanwhile, cook the pasta in a large pan of lightly salted boiling water for the time stated on the pack. Drain well.

3. Preheat the grill. Add the cheese sauce to the pasta with the mustard, chicken mixture and parsley. Mix well, then tip into a 2.1 litre (3¾ pint) ovenproof dish and sprinkle with Parmesan. Grill for 4–5 minutes until golden.

Serves 4

Best Bolognese

Hands-on time: 25 minutes
Cooking time: 1 hour

2 glugs of oil, such as olive, vegetable or sunflower

250g mushrooms, chopped

500g beef mince

1 glass red wine (optional)

1 × quantity All-round Tomato Sauce (see page 57)

few dashes Worcestershire sauce

2 large carrots, ends removed, coarsely grated

1 beef stock cube

To serve

cooked pasta

Cheddar or Parmesan, grated

SAVVY SWAP

For non-meat eaters use veggie mince and stock, and leave out the Worcestershire sauce.

1 Heat 1 glug of oil in a large pan over a high heat and fry the mushrooms, stirring occasionally, until soft and any liquid in the pan has evaporated, about 5 minutes. Empty the mushrooms into a bowl. Add another glug of oil to the pan, then add the mince. Stir to break it down and continue cooking until it's nicely browned.

2 Stir in the wine, if you like. Bring to the boil, then reduce the heat to medium and simmer until most of the liquid has evaporated.

3 Add the Tomato Sauce, Worcestershire sauce, carrots and cooked mushrooms. Crumble in the stock cube. Bring to the boil, then cover, reduce the heat and simmer for 45 minutes, stirring occasionally.

4 Serve with cooked pasta, topped with grated cheese.

Serves 6

Tuna Melt Pasta Bake

Hands-on time: 20 minutes
Cooking time: about 1 hour

4 standard mugfuls of dried penne
  or fusilli pasta
1 × quantity All-round Tomato Sauce
  (see page 57)
400g can chopped tomatoes
2 × 130g cans tuna, drained
a handful of pitted black olives, halved
3 × 25g pack ready-salted crisps,
  lightly crushed
1–2 large handfuls of Cheddar, grated
salt and freshly ground black pepper

1 Preheat the oven to 200°C
  (180°C fan oven) mark 6. Bring a
  large pan of water to the boil and
  cook the pasta for the time stated
  on the pack.

2 Meanwhile, empty the tomato sauce
  and the can of tomatoes into a
  separate large pan and bring to
  the boil. Take off the heat and put
  to one side.

3 Drain the pasta, then stir it into the
  tomato sauce with the tuna, olives
  and some seasoning.

4 Spoon the mixture into an
  ovenproof dish or roasting tin.
  Sprinkle the crisps and grated
  cheese over the top and cook in
  the oven for 35 minutes or until
  the cheese is bubbling and golden.
  Serve immediately.

Serves 6

Lasagne

Hands-on time: 1 hour
Cooking time: about 2 hours

1 glug of oil, such as vegetable, olive
   or sunflower
250g pack mushrooms, chopped
1 × quantity Best Bolognese sauce
   (see page 66)
1 medium carrot, ends removed,
   coarsely grated
2 × quantity White Sauce
   (see page 58)
2 large handfuls of Cheddar,
   coarsely grated
9 dried lasagne sheets
salt and freshly ground black pepper

SAVVY SWAP

You can also use white sauce
as a base for a fish pie, or stir
in grated cheese, mustard or
herbs and use it as a sauce for
fish or chicken.

1 Preheat the oven to 200°C (180°C
   fan oven) mark 6. Heat the oil
   in a large pan over a high heat
   and fry the mushrooms, stirring
   occasionally, until soft and any
   liquid in the pan has evaporated,
   about 5 minutes. Stir in the
   Bolognese Sauce and grated
   carrot and heat until bubbling.
   Put to one side.

2 Next, in a separate pan make the
   White Sauce. When it's ready, stir
   through half the cheese. Check
   the seasoning.

3 Spoon a third of the Bolognese into
   a large ovenproof dish, then top with
   3 lasagne sheets. Next, spoon over
   a third of the White Sauce. Repeat
   the layers with the remaining
   Bolognese, lasagne sheets and
   White Sauce until you have three
   complete layers. Sprinkle over the
   remaining grated cheese. Cook in
   the oven for 40-45 minutes until the
   top is golden and bubbling.

Serves 6

Cheat's Macaroni Cheese

Hands-on time: 10 minutes
Cooking time: about 10 minutes

300g (11oz) dried macaroni
300g pack cauliflower and broccoli florets (or ½ small head each broccoli and cauliflower), cut into smaller florets
300g (11oz) low-fat cream cheese
150g (5oz) mature Cheddar, grated
½ tsp English mustard
1 tbsp freshly chopped chives, plus extra to garnish
25g (1oz) dried breadcrumbs
salt and freshly ground black pepper
green salad to serve

1 Bring a large pan of water to the boil and cook the pasta for the time stated on the pack. Add the vegetables for the last 3 minutes. Drain and put back into the pan.

2 Meanwhile, put the cream cheese and most of the Cheddar into a small pan and heat gently to melt, then stir in the mustard, chives and some salt and ground black pepper. Stir the sauce into the drained pasta pan and check the seasoning. Add a little water if you like a thinner sauce.

3 Preheat the grill to medium. Divide the macaroni mixture among four individual heatproof dishes, then put them on a baking sheet. Sprinkle the remaining cheese and the breadcrumbs over the dishes, then season with pepper. Grill for 5 minutes or until golden and bubbling. Garnish with chives and serve with a green salad.

Serves 4

Home Comforts

Kitchen Smarts

Following a recipe is actually quite easy because the instructions take you through step by step. These tips and shortcuts will help you along the way.

Top Tips

- Read the recipe through quickly to make sure you understand it and have enough time to make it.
- Check that you have all the necessary ingredients.
- Check that you have the pans and other equipment.
- Clear the decks in the kitchen to give yourself room to work.
- Ingredients are listed in order of use but you don't need to prepare everything in one go. You can chop the onions, say, for the first step and while they're cooking prepare meat or more veg. But if cooking a stir-fry, prepare all the ingredients in one go, as it's a very fast cooking method.
- Take your time at each recipe step before moving on to the next one.
- Use a timer if you have one, or the alarm on your mobile phone – it's easy to lose track of time.
- Stay in the kitchen while cooking – a pan full of hot fat can be dangerous if it flares up.
- Clear up as you go along.

Top four recipe shortcuts

1 Don't bother with the garnishes.
2 Do use dried herbs instead of fresh if they are being cooked in the dish, but if they are to be added at the end they need to be fresh.
3 If you've only got a green pepper when it should be red, it's OK to use, but the flavour will alter a little.
4 If you don't have all the veg listed, use more of the ones you do have.

Savvy Shopping

It's all too easy to buy what you don't need or forget to buy what you do need, so it's worth having some kind of routine before you go shopping.

Before you go shopping

Do a quick weekly stocktake of the storecupboard, fridge and freezer, see what ingredients are close to their use-by dates, then think about how they can be incorporated into dishes over the next few days. Look at the recipes in this book and see what you need to buy to make the date-challenged ingredients into something tasty.

Plan meals for the week

· It's well worth having an idea of what you intend to eat for each day of the following week. Include some dishes that you've already made and frozen.
· Rethink your approach to cooking – meat and fish are expensive, so make two nights a week vegetarian.
· Plan to have meals with salad earlier in the week rather than later, as it doesn't last as well as some other vegetables.
· Bear in mind that you may want to change your plan if you find a bargain in the supermarket.

Top four shopping tips

1 Mostly stick to your shopping list and only buy special offers if you think you'll use them.
2 Buy seasonal foods (see pages 124–127).
3 If you have a freezer, buy larger amounts of meat or poultry and freeze portions, especially if they are on offer.
4 Compare the price per kilo. Loose fruit and veg can cost less than pre-packed versions, for example.

Foolproof Roast Chicken

Hands-on time: 25 minutes
Cooking time: about 1 hour 40 minutes

1 garlic bulb
4 fresh rosemary or thyme sprigs
50g (2oz) butter, softened
1 medium chicken, about 1.6kg (3½lb)
1 lemon
750g (1lb 11oz) baby new potatoes
1 tbsp plain flour
300ml (½ pint) chicken stock
1 tbsp caramelised onion relish
  or chutney
double cream (optional)
salt and freshly ground black pepper

1 Preheat the oven to 190°C (170°C fan oven) mark 5. Crush 1 garlic clove and put it into a small bowl. Pick the leaves from half the herb sprigs, roughly chop and add to the garlic bowl with the butter and plenty of seasoning. Stir together until combined.

2 Lift up the neck flap of the chicken and use your fingers to ease the skin gently away from the breast meat – work all the way down the sides of the breasts and towards the legs. Push half the butter mixture between the skin and the meat to cover the whole breast area. Pull the neck flap down and secure with a skewer or cocktail sticks. Halve the lemon and place one half in the cavity of the chicken, then tie the legs together. Cut the other half into wedges and put to one side.

3 Put the chicken into a large, sturdy roasting tin. Rub the remaining butter all over the outside of the chicken. Season well and roast for 45 minutes. Roughly bruise the remaining garlic cloves (do not peel) and add to the tin with the potatoes, lemon wedges and remaining herb sprigs, then shake to coat in the oil and put back into the oven for another 45 minutes or until the chicken and potatoes are cooked through.

4 Carefully transfer the chicken to a board and the potatoes, garlic and

78

lemon to a serving dish. Cover both well with foil. Spoon off and discard all but 1 tbsp fat from the roasting tin and heat it on the hob over a medium heat. Stir in the flour, cook for 1 minute, then gradually stir in the stock. Bubble for 5 minutes until thickened, stirring continuously.

Strain into a jug and stir in the onion relish or chutney and a little cream, if you like, if the gravy tastes too sharp. Season to taste.

5 Allow the chicken to rest for at least 30 minutes before serving with the potato mix, garlic and gravy (reheat the gravy if necessary).

Simple Chicken Casserole

Hands-on time: 10 minutes
Cooking time: about 1½ hours

4–6 chicken joints
3 tbsp oil
1 onion, chopped
2 garlic cloves, crushed
2 celery sticks, chopped
2 carrots, chopped
1 tbsp plain flour
2 tbsp freshly chopped tarragon or
thyme or 1 tsp dried
450ml (¾ pint) chicken stock
(see Take Stock)
salt and freshly ground black pepper

1 Preheat the oven to 180°C (160°C fan oven) mark 4. Cut the chicken legs and breasts in half.

2 Heat the oil in a flameproof casserole and brown the chicken all over. Remove and pour off the excess oil. Add the onion and garlic and brown for a few minutes. Add the vegetables, then stir in the flour and cook for 1 minute. Add the herbs and seasoning, and then add the chicken joints.

3 Pour enough stock into the casserole to come three-quarters of the way up the chicken – you might not need it all, or you might need to add a little extra water. Cook in the oven for 1–1½ hours until the chicken is cooked through.

TAKE STOCK

You can use 1 chicken stock cube dissolved in 450ml (¾ pint) boiling water.

SAVVY SWAP

If you don't have a flameproof casserole, start everything off in a frying pan, then transfer to the casserole and put in the oven.

Serves 4-6

Lamb Chops with Crispy Garlic Potatoes

Hands-on time: 10 minutes
Cooking time: 20 minutes

2 tbsp mint sauce
8 small lamb chops
3 medium potatoes, peeled and cut into 5mm (¼in) slices
2 tbsp garlic-flavoured olive oil
1 tbsp olive oil
salt and freshly ground black pepper
steamed green beans to serve

1 Spread the mint sauce over the lamb chops and leave to marinate while you prepare the potatoes.

2 Boil the potatoes in a pan of lightly salted water for 2 minutes or until just starting to soften. Drain, tip back into the pan, season and toss through the garlic oil.

3 Meanwhile, heat the olive oil in a large frying pan and fry the chops for 4–5 minutes on each side until just cooked, adding a splash of boiling water to the pan to make a sauce. Remove the chops and sauce from the pan and keep warm.

4 Add the potatoes to the pan. Fry over a medium heat for 10–12 minutes until crisp and golden. Divide the potatoes, chops and sauce among four plates and serve with green beans.

82

Serves 4

Shepherd's Pie

🍴 **Hands-on time:** 20 minutes
🍴 **Cooking time:** about 55 minutes

2 tbsp sunflower oil
450g (1lb) minced lamb
1 large onion, chopped
50g (2oz) mushrooms, sliced
2 carrots, chopped
2 tbsp plain flour
1 tbsp tomato purée
1 bay leaf (optional)
300ml (½ pint) lamb stock
　(see Take Stock)
700g (1½lb) potatoes, peeled and
　cut into large chunks
25g (1oz) butter
60ml (2¼fl oz) milk
50g (2oz) Cheddar, crumbled
　(optional)
green vegetables to serve

TAKE STOCK

You can use 1 lamb or vegetable stock cube dissolved in 300ml (½ pint) boiling water.

1 Heat half the oil in a large pan and brown the mince over a medium-high heat – do this in batches otherwise the meat will steam rather than fry. Remove with a slotted spoon on to a plate.

2 Reduce the heat to low and add the remaining oil. Gently fry the onion, mushrooms and carrots for 10 minutes or until softened. Stir in the flour and tomato purée and cook for 1 minute. Put the meat back into the pan and add the bay leaf, if you like. Pour in the stock and bring to the boil, then cover, reduce the heat and simmer over a low heat for 25 minutes.

3 Preheat the oven to 200°C (180°C fan oven) mark 6. Cook the potatoes in lightly salted boiling water for 20 minutes or until tender. Drain and leave in the colander for 2 minutes to steam dry. Melt the butter with the milk in the potato pan and add the potatoes. Mash until smooth.

Serves 4

4 Spoon the lamb mixture into a 1.7 litre (3 pint) casserole dish. Remove the bay leaf and check the seasoning. Cover with the mashed potato and sprinkle the cheese over, if you like. Bake for 15–20 minutes until bubbling and golden. Serve immediately with green vegetables.

Mini Toad in the Holes with Onion Gravy

Hands-on time: 15 minutes
Cooking time: 25 minutes

4 tbsp vegetable oil
12 pork sausages
3 large eggs
125g (4oz) plain flour
5 tbsp red onion marmalade
salt and freshly ground black pepper
mixed salad leaves or seasonal
   vegetables to serve

1 Preheat the oven to 220°C (200°C fan oven) mark 7. Heat 1 tbsp oil in a large frying pan and fry the sausages for 5 minutes or until just turning golden.

2 Divide 3 tbsp oil equally among the holes of a 12-hole deep muffin tin, then put one browned sausage into each hole. Put the tin into the oven to heat up. Put the frying pan to one side to reuse later.

3 In a large bowl, whisk together the eggs and flour to make a thick paste. Gradually whisk in 225ml (8fl oz) water and some seasoning to make a smooth batter. Transfer the mixture to a jug. Remove the tin from the oven and, working quickly, divide the batter among the holes. Put the tin back into the oven and cook for 20 minutes or until the batter is puffed up and golden.

4 Meanwhile, put the frying pan back on to a medium heat and stir in 5 tbsp water. Bubble for 30 seconds, then add the red onion marmalade and cook for 1 minute to make a thick gravy.

5 Serve the toad in the holes with gravy and mixed salad leaves or seasonal vegetables.

Serves 6

Healthy Ham, Egg and Chips

Hands-on time: 15 minutes
Cooking time: about 55 minutes

3 medium potatoes, skin on and
    cut into 2cm (¾in) dice

1 onion, roughly chopped

1 tbsp olive oil

400g (14oz) small closed cup
    mushrooms, halved if large

4 fresh thyme sprigs

250g (9oz) cherry tomatoes

1 tbsp wholegrain mustard

4 large eggs

125g (4oz) pulled ham hock
    (see Savvy Swap)

salt and freshly ground black pepper

freshly chopped parsley or chives to
    garnish (optional)

SAVVY SWAP

Pulled ham hock is now available
from some supermarkets but if
you can't find it, just shred some
thickly sliced ham.

1 Preheat the oven to 200°C (180°C
    fan oven) mark 6. In a large non-
    stick roasting tin (if you don't
    have non-stick, line with baking
    parchment) toss the potato cubes,
    onion, oil and plenty of seasoning.
    Roast for 20 minutes.

2 Take the tin out of the oven, add the
    mushrooms and thyme and toss
    together. Put the tin back into the
    oven for 25 minutes or until the veg
    are tender and golden.

3 Take the tin out of the oven again
    and toss through the cherry
    tomatoes and mustard. Make four
    spaces in the tin and break in the
    eggs. Put the tin back into the oven
    for 8–10 minutes until the egg whites
    are cooked. Top with the ham and
    herbs, if you like, and serve.

Chilli con Carne

Hands-on time: 15 minutes
Cooking time: 40 minutes

1 tbsp olive oil
1 onion, finely chopped
2 garlic cloves, crushed
1 red pepper, seeded and chopped
450g (1lb) minced beef
2 tsp chilli powder, mild or hot
300ml (½ pint) beef stock
  (see Take Stock)
2 tbsp tomato purée
400g can chopped tomatoes
2 tbsp Worcestershire sauce
125g (4oz) button mushrooms, sliced
400g can red kidney beans, drained
  and rinsed
grated Cheddar (optional)
salt and freshly ground black pepper
rice, jacket potatoes or flour tortillas
  to serve

1 Heat the oil in a large pan, add the onion and fry over a medium heat for 15 minutes until softened, stirring occasionally. Add the garlic and cook for 1 minute, then add the red pepper and cook for another 5 minutes.

2 Add the mince and, as it browns, use a wooden spoon to break up the pieces. Stir in the chilli powder, stock and tomato purée to the browned mince, cover the pan with a lid and bring to the boil. Add the tomatoes, Worcestershire sauce and mushrooms and season well with salt and ground black pepper.

3 Bring back to the boil, then reduce the heat and simmer, stirring occasionally, for 15 minutes. Add the kidney beans and cook for another 5 minutes to heat through.

4 Grate some cheese over, if you like, then serve with either rice, jacket potatoes or tortillas.

TAKE STOCK

You can use 1 beef stock cube dissolved in 300ml (½ pint) boiling water.

Serves 4

Paprika Beef Stew

🍴 **Hands-on time:** 20 minutes
Cooking time: 1¼ hours

1 tbsp sunflower oil
750g (1lb 11oz) braising or stewing
   steak, excess fat trimmed, cut into
   2cm (¾in) cubes
25g (1oz) plain flour
1 red onion, roughly chopped
1 each red and green pepper,
   seeded and roughly chopped
1½ tsp paprika
5 tbsp tomato purée
500ml (17fl oz) beef stock
250g (9oz) long-grain rice
salt and freshly ground black pepper
fresh coriander or parsley to garnish
cream, to drizzle (optional)

1. Heat the oil in a large pan over a medium heat. Meanwhile, dust the beef with the flour, making sure every bit is coated. Brown the beef in the pan (do this in batches if necessary to avoid overcrowding the pan).

2. Once all the beef is browned and put back into the pan, add the onion, peppers, paprika and tomato purée and fry for 5 minutes. Pour in the stock, bring to the boil, then cover, reduce the heat and simmer for 1 hour or until the beef is tender. Take the lid off for the final 15 minutes of the cooking time, stirring occasionally.

3. When the beef has 15 minutes left to cook, boil the rice for the time stated on the pack.

4. Check the stew seasoning. Garnish the beef with the coriander or parsley and a drizzle of cream, if you like. Serve with the rice.

Serves 4

Vegetable Curry

Hands-on time: 5 minutes
Cooking time: 12 minutes

1 tbsp medium curry paste

227g can chopped tomatoes

150ml (¼ pint) hot vegetable stock
  (see Take Stock)

200g (7oz) vegetables, such
  as broccoli, courgettes and
  sugarsnap peas, roughly chopped

½ × 400g can chickpeas, drained
  and rinsed

wholemeal pitta and yogurt to serve

1 Heat the curry paste in a large heavy-based pan for 1 minute, stirring the paste to warm the spices. Add the tomatoes and hot stock. Bring to the boil, then reduce the heat to a simmer and add the vegetables. Simmer for 5–6 minutes until the vegetables are tender.

2 Stir in the chickpeas and heat for 1–2 minutes until hot. Serve the vegetable curry with a griddled wholemeal pitta and yogurt.

TAKE STOCK

You can use ½ vegetable stock cube dissolved in 150ml (¼ pint) boiling water.

Serves 1

Better than a Takeaway

Living on a Budget

You can eat well without spending a lot of money on food. Sometimes it takes a bit of planning ahead though. At other times it's just about saving any leftovers that you couldn't eat and heating them up on another day. Some of the tastiest meals are simple, straightforward and cheap; Pesto Risotto (page 134) is one example, and many are quick to prepare – essential for busy, starving students!

Six ways to save money

1 Get organised – make your list while you're actually in the house, and not on the road to the shops. Check what you need before you leave.

2 Plan ahead – think about meals that might be worth making in bulk – a curry or a pasta sauce, for example. Or make a batch of Bolognese sauce and eat half one night then turn the remainder into a chilli with a can of red kidney beans and a few chilli flakes for the next night.

3 Share your shopping bills with friends.

4 Shop sensibly (see page 77) – stick to your shopping list and look for special offers.

5 Use up your leftovers – reheat that small portion of pasta sauce leftover from dinner the previous day for a quick lunch.

6 Check out the market or supermarket at the end of the day and buy some marked-down foods, if you think you'll use them.

Cheaper than a takeaway

Takeaways can be pretty tasty, and there are definitely times when cooking really does seem too much like a chore, but when you're trying to keep costs down (and perhaps aiming to eat healthily as well) it's a good idea to have a think and see what you can make that's just as appealing. There are lots of recipes in this book that are quick and simple to prepare, so they're light on labour as well as costing less.

Lunches on the go

Although there's lots of choice for lunch on the high street, the costs add up. If you make your own lunches you'll save money. Use up leftovers in salads and sandwiches.

Soup

You can't beat a homemade soup for a nutritious and warming meal. Plus, they are cheap to make and perfect for using up leftover vegetables. Try Quick Winter Minestrone (page 38).

Friday night takeaway

Make your own takeaway alternative and it will save you money and taste fantastic. It won't take long to cook either; in fact, by the time you've ordered a meal from the local shop and picked it up or had it delivered, you could have whipped up one of the delicious recipes from this chapter.

Pizzas

Rather than buying a takeaway pizza, buy the bases and make your own. Spread some tomato purée over the base, then top with whatever you have in the fridge. Tuna, ham, chicken, sweetcorn, peppers, cheese and pineapple all make excellent toppings.

Chicken Tikka Masala

🍴 **Hands-on time:** 20 minutes
Cooking time: about 30 minutes

1 tbsp vegetable oil

1 large onion, finely sliced

2 tbsp tikka masala paste

2 tbsp tomato purée

500g (1lb 2oz) skinless chicken
   breasts, cut into bite-size pieces

400g can chopped tomatoes

2 tbsp mango chutney

100ml (3½fl oz) natural yogurt

100ml (3½fl oz) double cream

salt and freshly ground black pepper

a large handful of fresh coriander,
   roughly chopped, to garnish
   (optional)

rice or naan breads
   to serve (optional)

1 Heat the oil in a large pan (that has a tightly fitted lid). Add the onion and a pinch of salt and cook over a low heat, covered, for 20 minutes or until the onions are completely softened.

2 Take off the lid and stir in the tikka masala paste, tomato purée and chicken pieces. Fry for a few minutes, then add the tomatoes. Bring to the boil, reduce the heat and simmer for 8–10 minutes until the chicken is cooked through.

3 Stir in the chutney, yogurt and cream and heat through. Check the seasoning. Garnish with coriander, if using, and serve with rice or naan breads, if you like.

SAVVY SWAP

You can use a double quantity
of natural yogurt instead of the
double cream.

100

Serves 4

Spiced Lamb Kebabs with Crunchy Coleslaw

Hands-on time: 10 minutes
Cooking time: about 15 minutes

1 red onion

1 garlic clove, roughly chopped

1 tsp each ground cumin, coriander
and cayenne pepper

350g (12oz) lean lamb mince

a small handful of fresh mint,
roughly chopped

½ small red cabbage, finely shredded

150g (5oz) low-fat natural yogurt

juice of ½ lemon

1 tbsp tahini

4 pitta breads

2 large tomatoes, sliced

salt and freshly ground black pepper

lemon wedges to serve

1 Preheat the grill to medium.
Roughly chop half the onion.
Mix the roughly chopped onion,
garlic, spices, lamb mince, most of
the mint and plenty of seasoning
until combined.

2 Divide the mixture into eight
and form each piece into a patty.
Transfer the patties to a non-stick
baking tray and grill for 10–12
minutes, turning once, until
cooked through.

3 Finely slice the remaining onion
and put into a large bowl with the
shredded cabbage. In a small bowl,
whisk together the yogurt, lemon
juice, tahini and remaining mint.

4 Stir half of the yogurt dressing
through the cabbage mixture and
check the seasoning.

5 Toast the pittas and cut horizontally
through the middle to make
pockets. Bring the pittas, patties,
tomatoes, coleslaw, lemon wedges
and remaining dressing to the table
and let people tuck in.

Serves 4

American-style Hamburgers

Hands-on time: 20 minutes, plus chilling
Cooking time: 10 minutes

1kg (2¼lb) extra-lean minced beef
2 tsp salt
2 tbsp steak seasoning
6 large soft rolls, halved
sunflower oil to grease and brush
6 thin-cut cheese slices
4 small cocktail gherkins,
  sliced lengthways
6 tbsp mustard mayonnaise
6 lettuce leaves, such as frisée
4 large tomatoes, thickly sliced
2 small onions, sliced into thin rings
freshly ground black pepper

1 Put the minced beef into a large bowl and add the salt, steak seasoning and plenty of ground black pepper. Use your hands to mix these ingredients together thoroughly.

2 Use your hands to shape the mixture into six even-size patties. Cover with clingfilm and chill for at least 1 hour.

3 Heat a large griddle pan until it's really hot. Put the rolls, cut sides down, on the griddle and toast.

4 Lightly oil the griddle, ease the burgers out of the moulds and brush with oil. Cook over a medium heat for about 3 minutes, then turn the burgers over carefully. Put a slice of cheese and a few slices of gherkin on top of each and cook for another 3 minutes.

5 While the burgers are cooking, spread the mustard mayonnaise on the toasted side of the rolls. Add the lettuce, tomatoes and shallots. Put the burgers on top and sandwich with the other half-rolls.

Serves 6

Tex-mex Veggie Burgers

Hands-on time: 20 minutes
Cooking time: 10 minutes

410g can black-eyed beans, drained
  and rinsed
410g can kidney beans, drained
  and rinsed
150g (5oz) sweetcorn
2 tbsp sliced jalapeño peppers
a small handful of fresh coriander,
  plus extra to garnish
2 medium eggs
75g (3oz) fresh or dried
  white breadcrumbs
1 tbsp olive oil
salt and freshly ground black pepper

To serve
4 burger buns, toasted (optional)
1 avocado, peeled, stoned
  and thinly sliced
4 tsp soured cream
4 tsp tomato salsa

1 Briefly pulse the first five ingredients and plenty of seasoning with a hand blender until they are combined but still have a chunky texture. Empty into a large bowl and stir through the eggs and breadcrumbs. Form into four patties.

2 Heat the oil in a large non-stick frying pan and gently fry the patties for 8–10 minutes, carefully turning once, until golden and piping hot.

3 Serve the burgers on toasted buns, if you like, topped with avocado slices, a small dollop of soured cream and some tomato salsa.

Serves 4

Skinny Bean Tacos

Hands-on time: 15 minutes
Cooking time: about 10 minutes

2 × 400g cans chopped tomatoes
2 tsp runny honey
410g can cannellini beans, drained
  and rinsed
400g can kidney beans, drained
  and rinsed
198g can sweetcorn, drained
1 red onion, finely chopped
salt and freshly ground black pepper

To serve

8 corn tacos
reduced-fat guacamole
a large handful of fresh parsley
  leaves, chopped

1 Put the tomatoes into a medium pan with the honey and plenty of seasoning. Bring to the boil, then reduce the heat and simmer until thickened, about 8 minutes.

2 Stir in both types of beans, the sweetcorn, onion and some seasoning. Heat through and check the seasoning.

3 Warm the taco shells according to the pack instructions.

4 Put the bean mixture, tacos, guacamole and parsley into separate bowls, take to the table and let everyone serve themselves.

Serves 4

Naan Pizza

Hands-on time: 5 minutes
Cooking time: about 10 minutes

2 plain naans
2 tbsp caramelised red onion chutney
50g (2oz) soft goat's cheese, crumbled
75g (3oz) cherry tomatoes, quartered
2 fresh thyme sprigs, leaves picked
freshly ground black pepper
a small handful of rocket
extra virgin olive oil to drizzle
   (optional)
green salad to serve

1 Preheat the oven to 220°C (200°C fan oven) mark 7.
2 Put the naans on a baking sheet, then spread the onion chutney over them. Dot with the goat's cheese, tomatoes and thyme leaves, then season with ground black pepper.
3 Cook in the oven for 5–10 minutes until the cheese has softened and the pizza is piping hot.
4 Garnish with rocket leaves, drizzle with oil, if you like, and serve with a green salad.

Serves 2

Tuna Melt Pizza

Hands-on time: 5 minutes
Cooking time: about 12 minutes

2 large pizza bases
4 tbsp sun-dried tomato pesto or basil pesto
2 × 185g cans tuna, drained
50g can anchovies, drained and chopped
125g (4oz) mature Cheddar, grated
rocket to serve (optional)

1 Put two baking sheets in the oven on separate shelves and preheat the oven to 220°C (200°C fan oven) mark 7.

2 When the baking sheets have heated up, take them out of the oven (use oven gloves) and put a pizza base on each tray.

3 Spread each pizza base with 2 tbsp sun-dried tomato or basil pesto. Top each with half the tuna, half the anchovies and half the grated cheese. Put back into the oven and cook for 10–12 minutes until the cheese has melted. Sprinkle with rocket to serve, if you like.

SAVVY SWAP

For a ham and pineapple pizza, spread the pizza bases with 4 tbsp tomato pasta sauce. Top with a 225g can drained unsweetened pineapple chunks, 125g (4oz) diced ham and 125g (4oz) grated cheese.

Serves 4

Fish and Chips

🍴 **Hands-on time:** 15 minutes
Cooking time: about 40 minutes

4 large baking potatoes,
    about 900g (2lb)
3 tbsp vegetable oil
25g (1oz) plain flour
1 large egg, beaten
100g (3½oz) fresh white breadcrumbs
4 × 125g (4oz) cod fillets, skinned
450g (1lb) fresh or frozen peas
1½ tbsp finely sliced fresh mint
salt and freshly ground black pepper
tartare sauce, lemon wedges and
    malt vinegar to serve

1 Preheat the oven to 200°C (180°C fan oven) mark 6. Cut the potatoes into wedges and put on a large baking tray. Drizzle with 1½ tbsp of the oil, season and toss to coat the wedges. Cook in the oven for 30–40 minutes until tender and golden.

2 Put the flour, egg and breadcrumbs on to three separate lipped plates. When the wedges are 10 minutes away from being finished, bring a medium pan of water to the boil.

Meanwhile, coat each fish fillet in flour, then dip into the egg and then into the breadcrumbs.

3 Heat the remaining oil in a large, non-stick frying pan and cook the fish for 5 minutes, turning once, or until golden and cooked through.

4 Add the peas to the boiling water and cook for 2–3 minutes until tender. Drain.

5 Using a potato masher, roughly crush the peas, then stir in the mint and seasoning to taste.

6 Serve the fish with a dollop of tartare sauce and a lemon wedge, plus the potato wedges and peas, and malt vinegar to sprinkle over.

SAVVY SWAP

Frozen fish fillets keep costs down. Thaw them fully before using – in the fridge on a baking tray lined with kitchen paper.

Sweet and Sour Pork Stir-fry

Hands-on time: 15 minutes
Cooking time: about 10 minutes

2 tbsp vegetable oil
350g (12oz) pork fillet, cut into
   finger-size pieces
1 red onion, finely sliced
1 red pepper, seeded and finely sliced
2 carrots, cut into thin strips
3 tbsp sweet chilli sauce
1 tbsp white wine vinegar
220g can pineapple slices, chopped,
   with 2 tbsp juice put to one side
a large handful of bean sprouts
½ tbsp sesame seeds
a large handful of fresh coriander,
   roughly chopped
salt and freshly ground black pepper
boiled long-grain rice to serve

1 Heat the oil over a high heat in a large frying pan or wok. Add the pork, onion, red pepper and carrots and cook for 3–5 minutes, stirring frequently, until the meat is cooked through and the vegetables are softening.

2 Stir in the chilli sauce, vinegar and reserved pineapple juice and bring to the boil, then stir in the pineapple chunks and bean sprouts and heat through.

3 Check the seasoning. Sprinkle the sesame seeds and coriander over and serve immediately with rice.

COOK'S TRICK

Have all your ingredients sliced and ready before you start cooking.

Serves 4

Rice and Red Pepper Stir-fry

Hands-on time: 5 minutes
Cooking time: 15 minutes

75g (3oz) long-grain rice

200ml (7fl oz) hot vegetable stock

2 tsp vegetable oil

½ onion, thinly sliced

2 streaky bacon rashers, chopped

1 small red pepper, seeded and
  cut into chunks

a handful of frozen peas

1 dash Worcestershire sauce

1 Put the rice in a pan and pour over the hot stock. Cover, bring to the boil, reduce the heat and simmer for 10 minutes or until the rice is tender and the liquid has been absorbed.

2 Meanwhile, heat the oil in a wok or large frying pan over a medium heat. Add the onion slices and fry for 5 minutes. Add the bacon and pepper and fry for 5 minutes more or until the bacon is crisp.

3 Stir the cooked rice and the peas into the onion mixture and cook, stirring occasionally, for 2–3 minutes until the rice and peas are hot. Add a dash of Worcestershire sauce and serve immediately.

Serves 4

Clever leftovers

We all struggle with portion sizing and often have extra food at the end of each meal, but there are many ways of using up unwanted leftovers.

Ways of using leftovers

❑ Simply add the ingredients to a stir-fry, pasta bake, soup (see opposite) ... the list is endless

❑ Make the most of fruit and vegetables that are starting to wilt – use fruit in a crumble, use vegetables in soups and bakes

Stretching meals

Stretch the ingredients – sometimes the amount left over is so small it won't go very far on its own. Try adding to it:

❑ Add lentils and tomatoes to leftover mince to create a whole new take on Bolognese sauce

❑ Casseroles and stews usually include plenty of vegetables, so you can just serve with bread

❑ Add canned beans and pulses to bulk out stews and casseroles. Drain and rinse them first

❑ Cook dishes in bulk to save on fuel and then store in the fridge for up to three days or freeze them.

Freezing leftovers

You may not always feel like transforming your leftovers into meals – or there may not be enough to do so. Another option is to freeze the odd ingredient for later use.

❑ Small amounts of herbs – freeze in ice cube trays

❑ Chillies – these freeze well and are easy to chop from frozen

❑ Double cream – lightly whip the cream and then freeze

❑ Cheese – hard cheeses will become crumbly once thawed, but can be used for grating or in cooking

Basic Vegetable Soup
Serves 4

1 glug of oil – vegetable, olive
    or sunflower
1 onion, chopped
4 celery sticks, roughly chopped
4 carrots, chopped
2 potatoes, peeled and chopped
1 chicken or vegetable stock cube
salt and freshly ground black
    pepper
Cheddar, cubed (optional)
bread to serve

1 Heat the oil in a large pan over
a low-medium heat and add the
onion. Stir occasionally.

2 Add the chopped celery to the
pan and give the mixture a stir.

3 Add the carrots and potatoes to
the pan and continue to cook,
stirring occasionally, for
another 5 minutes.

4 Crumble the stock cube into a
standard-sized mug and fill with
boiling water. Stir to dissolve the
cube and pour into the pan. Add
three to four further mugfuls
of boiling water to your soup,
depending on how liquidy you
want it.

5 Turn up the heat until the soup
is boiling, then reduce the heat
and leave it to simmer gently
for 15 minutes – the surface
should be gently bubbling – until
the veg is tender. Check the
seasoning and ladle into bowls
or mugs. Top with cheese, if you
like, and serve with bread.

Food for Friends

Keep It Seasonal

Although you can buy most produce all year round, it's going to taste better and – more importantly when eating on a budget – it will be much cheaper when it's in season. Also, if you want to shop ethically and avoid environmentally damaging food miles, look out for local produce, which, of course, will be seasonal.

January
Vegetables Beetroot, Brussels sprouts, cauliflower, celeriac, celery, chicory, kale, leeks, parsnips, potatoes (maincrop), rhubarb, swede, turnips
Fruit Apples, clementines, kiwi fruit, lemons, oranges, passion fruit, pears, pineapple, pomegranate, satsumas, tangerines
Nuts Walnuts
Fish Haddock, hake, lemon sole, plaice

February
Vegetables Brussels sprouts, cauliflower, celeriac, chicory, kale, leeks, parsnips, potatoes (maincrop), rhubarb, swede
Fruit Bananas, blood oranges, kiwi fruit, lemons, oranges, passion fruit, pears, pineapple, pomegranate
Fish Cod, haddock, hake, lemon sole, salmon

March
Vegetables Cauliflower, chicory, kale, leeks, purple sprouting broccoli, rhubarb, spring onions
Fruit Bananas, blood oranges, kiwi fruit, lemons, oranges, passion fruit, pineapple, pomegranate
Fish Cod, hake, lemon sole, salmon, sea trout

April

Vegetables Broccoli, Jersey Royal potatoes, purple sprouting broccoli, radishes, rhubarb, rocket, spinach, spring onions, watercress
Fruit Bananas, kiwi fruit
Fish Cod, salmon, sea trout

May

Vegetables Broccoli, Jersey Royal potatoes, new potatoes, radishes, rhubarb, rocket, spinach, spring onions, watercress
Fruit Cherries, kiwi fruit, strawberries
Meat Lamb
Fish Cod, lemon sole, plaice, salmon, sea trout

June

Vegetables Aubergines, broad beans, broccoli, carrots, courgettes, mangetouts, Jersey Royal potatoes, new potatoes, peas, radishes, rocket, runner beans, spring onions, turnips, watercress
Fruit Cherries, strawberries
Meat Lamb
Fish Cod, haddock, herring, lemon sole, mackerel, plaice, salmon, sardines, sea trout

July

Vegetables Aubergines, beetroot, broad beans, broccoli, carrots, courgettes, cucumber, French beans, garlic, mangetouts, new potatoes, onions, peas, potatoes (maincrop), radishes, rocket, runner beans, turnips, watercress
Fruit Apricots, blackberries, blueberries, cherries, gooseberries, kiwi fruit, melons, peaches, raspberries, redcurrants, strawberries, tomatoes
Meat Lamb
Fish Cod, haddock, herring, lemon sole, mackerel, plaice, salmon, sardines, sea trout

August

Vegetables Aubergines, beetroot, broad beans, broccoli, carrots, courgettes, cucumber, French beans, garlic, leeks, mangetouts, marrow, new potatoes, onions, peas, peppers, potatoes (maincrop), radishes, rocket, runner beans, sweetcorn, watercress

Fruit Apricots, blackberries, blueberries, damsons, kiwi fruit, melons, nectarines, peaches, plums, raspberries, redcurrants, tomatoes

Meat Lamb

Fish Cod, haddock, herring, lemon sole, mackerel, plaice, salmon, sardines

September

Vegetables Aubergines, beetroot, broccoli, butternut squash, carrots, courgettes, cucumber, garlic, leeks, mangetouts, marrow, onions, parsnips, peas, peppers, potatoes (maincrop), radishes, rocket, runner beans, sweetcorn, watercress

Fruit Apples, blackberries, damsons, figs, grapes, melons, nectarines, peaches, pears, plums, raspberries, redcurrants, tomatoes

Nuts Walnuts

Meat Lamb

Fish Cod, haddock, herring, lemon sole, mackerel, plaice

October

Vegetables Beetroot, broccoli, butternut squash, carrots, celeriac, celery, kale, leeks, marrow, onions, parsnips, potatoes (maincrop), pumpkin, swede, turnips, watercress
Fruit Apples, chestnuts, figs, pears, quince, tomatoes
Nuts Walnuts
Fish Haddock, hake, lemon sole, mackerel, plaice

November

Vegetables Beetroot, Brussels sprouts, celeriac, celery, chicory, kale, leeks, parsnips, potatoes (maincrop), pumpkin, swede, turnips, watercress
Fruit Apples, chestnuts, clementines, cranberries, figs, passion fruit, pears, quince, satsumas, tangerines
Nuts Walnuts
Fish Haddock, hake, lemon sole, plaice

December

Vegetables Beetroot, Brussels sprouts, cauliflower, celeriac, celery, chicory, kale, leeks, parsnips, potatoes (maincrop), pumpkin, swede, turnips
Fruit Apples, chestnuts, clementines, cranberries, passion fruit, pears, pineapple, pomegranate, satsumas, tangerines
Nuts Walnuts
Fish Haddock, hake, lemon sole, plaice

Beercan Chicken

Hands-on time: 10 minutes
Cooking time: 1½ hours

1 tsp paprika

1 tsp dried mixed herbs

1 tbsp sunflower oil

1 medium chicken, about 1.6kg (3½lb)

440ml can lager

salt and freshly ground black pepper

coleslaw and a crisp green salad
  to serve

1 Take the shelves out of your oven, line the bottom with foil and preheat to 190°C (170°C fan oven) mark 5.

2 In a small bowl, stir together the paprika, dried herbs, oil and plenty of seasoning. Rub the mixture all over the outside of the chicken.

3 Open the lager and pour half into a glass (to enjoy later!). Put the half-filled can upright in the centre of a large, sturdy roasting tin, then sit the chicken, cavity side down, on top of it (the can should fill the cavity and the chicken should be upright).

4 Slowly slide the roasting tin into the oven. Roast the chicken for 1½ hours or until golden and cooked through. Carefully remove from the oven, cover lightly with foil and leave to rest on the can for 30 minutes.

5 Carefully pull the chicken off the can. Serve with coleslaw and a crisp green salad.

COOK'S TRICK

Make sure you have enough space in your oven and line it with foil.

Serves 4

Chicken Fajitas

Hands-on time: 15 minutes
Cooking time: 10 minutes

4 large flour tortilla wraps

2 tsp oil

1 garlic clove, crushed

½–1 tsp smoked paprika, to taste

2 tbsp tomato purée

1 tsp runny honey

4 cooked skinless chicken breasts,
   cut into finger-size strips

125g (4oz) roasted red peppers from
   a jar, drained and sliced

a large handful of fresh coriander,
   chopped

salt and freshly ground black pepper

To serve (optional)

guacamole

soured cream

grated Cheddar

1 Stack the tortillas, then wrap in foil. Put into the oven, then turn the oven on to 200°C (180°C fan oven) mark 6 (no need to preheat, as you're just warming the tortillas). Alternatively, wrap the tortillas in clingfilm and microwave on full power for 30-second bursts until warmed through.

2 Meanwhile, heat the oil in a large frying pan, add the garlic and paprika and fry for 30 seconds, then stir in the tomato purée, honey and 4 tbsp water. Add the chicken and sliced peppers and simmer for 5 minutes or until piping hot. Stir in most of the coriander and check the seasoning.

3 Spoon the chicken mixture into a dish and garnish with the remaining coriander. Serve the mixture with the warmed tortillas, the guacamole, soured cream and grated cheese, if you like, and let everyone tuck in.

Serves 4

Turkey Meatballs with Barbecue Sauce

Hands-on time: 15 minutes
Cooking time: about 20 minutes

500g (1lb 2oz) turkey mince
2 tsp ground coriander
½–1 red chilli, seeded and finely
  chopped (see Safety Tip, page 28)
½ tbsp olive oil
1 onion, finely chopped
1 garlic clove, crushed
400g can chopped tomatoes
2 tbsp soy sauce
3 tbsp tomato ketchup
salt and freshly ground black pepper
fresh coriander, chives or parsley
  to garnish (optional)
boiled wholegrain rice to serve

1 Preheat the oven to 200°C (180°C
  fan oven) mark 6 and line a baking
  tray with baking parchment.
2 Put the turkey mince into a large
  bowl, add the ground coriander,
  chilli and plenty of seasoning and
  mix through (using your hands
  is easiest). Form into walnut-size
  meatballs – you should have
  about 20.
3 Arrange the meatballs on the
  prepared tray and cook in the oven,
  turning midway, for 20 minutes or
  until golden and cooked through.
4 Meanwhile, heat the oil in a large
  pan over a medium heat. Add the
  onion and fry for 10 minutes or until
  softened. Stir in the garlic and cook
  for 1 minute, then add the tomatoes,
  soy sauce, ketchup and seasoning.
  Bring to the boil, then reduce the
  heat and simmer for 10 minutes or
  until thickened slightly.
5 Add the meatballs to the sauce and
  stir gently to coat. Garnish with
  fresh herbs, if you like, and serve
  with boiled wholegrain rice.

Serves 4

Pesto Risotto

Hands-on time: 15 minutes
Cooking time: about 30 minutes

1 glug of oil, such as vegetable, olive or sunflower

1 onion, finely chopped

1½ standard mugfuls of risotto rice, such as arborio or carnaroli

1 chicken or vegetable stock cube

pesto to taste

1 standard mugful of frozen peas

200g pack ham, chopped

salt and freshly ground black pepper

COOK'S TRICK

For a tasty lunch, cool leftover risotto quickly, then cover it with clingfilm or foil and chill it as soon as it gets to room temperature. Keep it in the fridge for up to two days. It should be dry and quite sticky, so you can shape it into burger-size patties. Heat a glug of oil in a frying pan and fry the patties for 10 minutes, turning once, until piping hot. Serve topped with fried eggs.

1 Heat the oil in a large pan over a medium heat and add the onion. Fry for 10 minutes, stirring occasionally, or until the onion is translucent.

2 Add the rice and give the mixture a good stir to prevent it from sticking.

3 Crumble the stock cube into a standard-sized mug and fill it with boiling water from the kettle. Stir to dissolve the cube and pour it into the rice saucepan. Add three further mugfuls of boiling water.

4 When the liquid in the pan starts to boil, reduce the heat to low and cook for 15–20 minutes, occasionally stirring well, until the rice absorbs the liquid. Add half a mugful of boiling water if all the liquid has disappeared but the rice still isn't cooked and cook it for a little longer. Repeat until the rice is tender.

5 Stir in the pesto (as much as you want), frozen peas and ham and continue cooking until the peas are hot. Check the seasoning and serve.

Serves 4

Hangover Ham and Veg Pie

Hands-on time: 20 minutes
Cooking time: about 50 minutes

1 × quantity Basic Vegetable Soup made up to step 3 (see page 121)
3 × quantity White Sauce (see page 58)
200g pack ham or any leftover meats you have (chicken and sausage work well), chopped
320g pack ready-rolled puff pastry
salt and freshly ground black pepper

1 Preheat the oven to 200°C (180°C fan oven) mark 6. Cook the vegetables in the soup mix for 10 minutes more until they are cooked through.

2 Stir in the White Sauce and ham or leftover meats. Check the seasoning (it will need a fair amount). Pour the mixture into an ovenproof serving dish or roasting tin. Unroll the puff pasty and lay it on top of the mixture, pressing it on to the sides of the dish or tin to seal.

3 Cut a 2.5cm (1in) cross in the middle of the pastry to let the steam escape and cook it in the oven for 30 minutes or until the pastry is golden. Serve immediately.

SAVVY SWAP

If you are cooking for non-meat eaters, make up the soup with vegetable stock and add a large handful of peas instead of the ham.

Serves 6

Mediterranean Sausage One-pot

Hands-on time: 15 minutes
Cooking time: 40 minutes

8 pork sausages
1 red onion, cut into 8 wedges
1 tbsp roughly chopped oregano or
    ½ tbsp dried oregano, plus extra
    to garnish
5 garlic cloves, skin on
3 medium sweet potatoes, about 500g
    (1lb 2oz), cut into 2.5cm (1in) chunks
2 tbsp extra virgin olive oil
3 tomatoes, cut into wedges
50g (2oz) black olives, pitted
salt and freshly ground black pepper
crusty bread to serve (optional)

1 Preheat the oven to 200°C (180°C fan oven) mark 6. Put the sausages into a large roasting tin and add the onion wedges, oregano, garlic, sweet potatoes, oil and plenty of seasoning. Toss everything together, then roast for 30 minutes.

2 Add the tomato wedges and black olives and put back into the oven for 10 minutes. Garnish with extra oregano and serve with some crusty bread, if you like.

COOK'S TRICK

Buy good-quality sausages, so they brown nicely and don't split and burst.

Serves 4

Mexican Beef Bake

Hands-on time: 15 minutes
Cooking time: about 30 minutes

1 tbsp sunflower oil

1 large onion, finely chopped

500g pack beef mince

1–2 green chillies, seeded
and finely chopped (see Safety Tip,
page 28)

400g can chopped tomatoes

410g can kidney beans, drained
and rinsed

a large handful of fresh coriander,
roughly chopped

100g (3½oz) tortilla chips
(lightly salted)

50g (2oz) mature Cheddar, grated

salt and freshly ground black pepper

soured cream and a crisp green salad
to serve

1 Heat the oil in a large pan and
gently cook the onion until softened,
about 10 minutes. Turn up the heat
and stir in the beef and cook until
all the meat is well browned, about
10 minutes.

2 Add the chillies, tomatoes, kidney
beans and plenty of seasoning
and cook for 5 minutes. Stir in the
coriander and check the seasoning.
Empty the mixture into a heatproof
serving dish.

3 Preheat the grill to medium. Top
the beef mixture with the tortilla
chips and cheese. Grill until it is
piping hot and the cheese is melted
and golden.

4 Serve immediately with soured
cream and a crisp green salad.

COOK'S TRICK

Prepare to the end of step 2,
cover and store in the fridge until
needed. To serve, reheat the chilli
beef, then continue with step 3.

140

Serves 4

Halloumi Kebabs

Hands-on time: 15 minutes, plus soaking
Cooking time: about 10 minutes

1 large courgette, trimmed and
   cut into chunks
1 red pepper, seeded and cut
   into chunks
12 cherry tomatoes
125g (4oz) halloumi cheese, cubed
100g (3½oz) natural yogurt
1 tsp ground cumin
2 tbsp olive oil
squeeze of lemon
1 lemon, cut into 8 wedges
couscous tossed with freshly
   chopped flat-leafed parsley
   to serve (see Cook's Trick)

1 Preheat the barbecue or grill. Soak
  eight wooden skewers in water for
  20 minutes.
2 Put the courgette into a large
  bowl with the red pepper, cherry
  tomatoes and halloumi cheese. Add
  the yogurt, cumin, oil and a squeeze
  of lemon and mix.

3 Push a lemon wedge on to each
  skewer, then divide the vegetables
  and cheese among the skewers.
  Grill the kebabs, turning regularly,
  for 8–10 minutes until the vegetables
  are tender and the halloumi is nicely
  charred. Serve with couscous.

COOK'S TRICK

To make couscous, measure
the couscous in a bowl and add
1½ times the volume of hot water
or stock. Cover the bowl and
leave to soak for 5 minutes. Fluff
up with a fork before serving.
If using for a salad, leave the
couscous to cool completely
before adding the other salad
ingredients.

Serves 4

Aubergine, Chickpea and Sweet Potato Curry

Hands-on time: 20 minutes
Cooking time: 35 minutes

2 tbsp olive oil

1 large onion, thinly sliced

1 tbsp each garam masala and
  black onion seeds

1½ tsp turmeric

5cm (2in) fresh root ginger, peeled
  and grated

2 garlic cloves, crushed

1 large aubergine, cut into
  2cm (¾in) cubes

2 medium sweet potatoes, cut into
  2cm (¾in) cubes

2 × 400g cans chopped tomatoes

410g can chickpeas, drained and
  rinsed

large handful of fresh coriander, roughly
  chopped, plus extra to garnish

salt and freshly ground black pepper

boiled rice to serve

1 Heat the oil in a large pan over
  medium heat. Add the onion and
  cook for 10 minutes until softened.
  Stir in the garam masala, black
  onion seeds, turmeric, ginger and
  garlic and cook for 1 minute.

2 Stir in the aubergine and sweet
  potatoes and fry for 5 minutes.
  Add the tomatoes and simmer for
  15 minutes, stirring occasionally, or
  until the vegetables are tender.

3 Stir in the chickpeas and chopped
  coriander, then check the seasoning.
  Serve with boiled rice, garnished
  with extra coriander.

FREEZE AHEAD

Prepare the curry to the end of
step 2, cool, then transfer to a
container and freeze for up to
one month. To serve, thaw in the
fridge then reheat gently in pan.
Complete the recipe to serve.

Peppers Stuffed with Mushrooms

Hands-on time: 20 minutes
Cooking time: about 50 minutes

40g (1½oz) butter

4 red peppers, halved and seeded, leaving the stalks intact

3 tbsp olive oil

350g (12oz) mushrooms, roughly chopped (chestnut mushrooms are good)

4 tbsp freshly chopped chives

100g (3½oz) feta cheese

50g (2oz) fresh white breadcrumbs

25g (1oz) freshly grated Parmesan

salt and freshly ground black pepper

1 Preheat the oven to 180°C (160°C fan oven) mark 4. Use a little of the butter to grease a shallow ovenproof dish, then put in the peppers side by side, hollow side up.

2 Heat the remaining butter and 1 tbsp of the oil in a pan. Add the mushrooms and fry until they are golden and there's no excess liquid left in the pan. Stir in the chives, then spoon the mixture into the pepper halves.

3 Crumble the feta cheese over the mushrooms. Mix the breadcrumbs and Parmesan in a bowl, then sprinkle the mixture over the top.

4 Season with salt and ground black pepper and drizzle with the remaining oil. Roast for 45 minutes or until golden and tender. Serve warm.

Sweet Treats

Cornershop Cheat's Chocolate Mousse

Hands-on time: 15 minutes
Cooking time: 5 minutes, plus cooling

125g (4oz) marshmallows

50g (2oz) butter

200g bar plain chocolate, broken
  into pieces

300ml tub double cream

Crunchie bars, crushed,
  to decorate (optional)

1 Put the marshmallows, butter, chocolate and 4 tbsp water into a pan and heat over a low heat (stirring constantly) until melted and smooth (do not allow the mixture to bubble and overheat). Take off the heat and stir for 30 seconds – it should be thick and very shiny. Leave to cool for 20–30 minutes (no more). The mixture should be at room temperature.

2 When your chocolate has cooled, pour the cream into a large bowl and whip it with a whisk or fork until you can lift the whisk or fork out and the cream will stay in a soft mound.

3 Use a big spoon to scrape the chocolate into the cream and gently stir everything together (stirring too hard will make the mousse heavy). Spoon into glasses or bowls, top with crumbled Crunchie bars, if you like, and serve.

Eton Mess

200g (7oz) fromage frais, chilled

200g (7oz) low-fat Greek yogurt, chilled

1 tbsp golden caster sugar

2 tbsp strawberry liqueur (optional)

6 meringues, roughly crushed

350g (12oz) strawberries, hulled and halved

1 Put the fromage frais and yogurt into a large bowl and stir to combine.

2 Add the sugar, meringues, strawberries and strawberry liqueur, if you like. Mix together gently and divide among six serving dishes.

Serves 6

Strawberry and Cream Jelly

Hands-on time: 20 minutes, plus chilling and setting
Cooking time: 5 minutes

2 × 135g packs strawberry jelly
¹/₈ tsp edible gold glitter (optional)
oil to grease (optional)
100g (3½oz) caster sugar
½ tsp vanilla extract
300ml (½ pint) double cream
600ml (1 pint) milk
8 gelatine sheets

1 Snip the jelly into cubes and put into a large jug. Pour over 300ml (½ pint) boiling water and leave to dissolve, stirring occasionally. Top up the mixture with cold water until there is 1.2 litres (2¹/₈ pints). Stir in the glitter, if you like.

2 Pour the strawberry jelly mixture into a 2.7 litres (4¾ pints) non-stick kugelhopf mould or large bowl (if your bowl or mould is not non-stick, grease lightly with a mild oil). Chill until completely set, about 3 hours.

3 Meanwhile, put the sugar, vanilla extract, cream and milk into a pan and heat gently, whisking occasionally, until the mixture just begins to boil. Take off the heat and leave for 15 minutes.

4 Put the gelatine sheets into a bowl and cover with cold water. Leave to soak for 5 minutes. Lift the gelatine out of the water and add to the cream pan – stir to dissolve (if the cream mixture is not hot enough to dissolve the gelatine, then reheat gently until it dissolves). Leave the mixture until completely cool – the strawberry jelly needs to be fully set before proceeding.

5 Gently pour the cream mixture over the set jelly and refrigerate to set completely, about 5 hours.

6 Turn out the jelly on to a plate. If it doesn't come out easily, dip the base of the mould briefly into a bowl of hot water (taking care no water comes in contact with the jelly).

Serves 10

COOK'S TRICK

Make the jelly to the end of step 5 up to two days ahead. Chill. Complete the recipe to serve.

Apple Compote

Hands-on time: 10 minutes, plus chilling
Cooking time: 5 minutes

250g (9oz) cooking apples, peeled, cored and chopped
juice of ½ lemon
1 tbsp golden caster sugar
ground cinnamon

To serve
25g (1oz) raisins
25g (1oz) chopped almonds
1 tbsp natural yogurt

1 Put the apples into a pan with the lemon juice, sugar and 2 tbsp cold water. Cook gently for 5 minutes or until soft.
2 Transfer to a bowl. Sprinkle a little ground cinnamon over the top and chill. It will keep for up to three days.
3 Serve with the raisins, chopped almonds and yogurt.

SAVVY SWAP

If you've got a microwave, put the apples, lemon juice, sugar and water into a microwave-safe bowl, cover loosely with clingfilm and cook on full power in an 850W microwave for 4 minutes until the apple is just soft.

Serves 2

Pear and Blackberry Crumble

🍴 **Hands-time:** 20 minutes
Cooking time: about 45 minutes

450g (1lb) pears, peeled, cored
  and chopped, tossed with the
  juice of 1 lemon
225g (8oz) golden caster sugar
1 tsp mixed spice
450g (1lb) blackberries
cream, custard or ice cream to serve

For the crumble topping
100g (3½oz) butter, chopped,
  plus extra to grease
225g (8oz) plain flour
75g (3oz) ground almonds

1 Put the pears and lemon juice into
  a bowl, add 100g (3½oz) sugar
  and the mixed spice, then add the
  blackberries and toss thoroughly
  to coat.
2 Preheat the oven to 200°C (180°C
  fan oven) mark 6. Lightly grease a
  1.8 litre (3¼ pint) shallow ovenproof
  dish, then carefully tip the fruit into
  the dish in an even layer.
3 To make the crumble topping, rub
  the butter into the flour in a large
bowl by hand. Stir in the ground
almonds and the remaining sugar.
Bring parts of the mixture together
with your hands to make lumps.
4 Spoon the crumble topping evenly
  over the fruit, then put into the oven
  and bake for 35–45 minutes until
  the fruit is tender and the crumble
  is golden and bubbling. Serve with
  cream, custard or ice cream.

SAVVY SWAP

Crumble is a great way to use
leftover, slightly overripe fruit.
Replace the pears with apples, or
omit the blackberries and use
700g (1½lb) plums or rhubarb
instead. You could also use
gooseberries (omit the spice),
or try 450g (1lb) rhubarb with
450g (1lb) strawberries.

Serves 6

Bread and Butter Pudding

Hands-on time: 10 minutes, plus soaking
Cooking time: about 40 minutes

50g (2oz) butter, softened, plus extra
  to grease
275g (10oz) white loaf, cut into 1cm
  (½in) slices, crusts removed
50g (2oz) raisins or sultanas
3 medium eggs
450ml (¾ pint) milk
3 tbsp golden icing sugar,
  plus extra to dust

1 Lightly grease four 300ml (½ pint)
  gratin dishes or one 1.1 litre (2 pint)
  ovenproof dish.

2 Butter the bread, then cut into
  quarters to make triangles. Arrange
  the bread in the dish(es) and
  sprinkle with the raisins or sultanas.

3 Beat the eggs, milk and sugar in
  a bowl. Pour the mixture over
  the bread and leave to soak for
  10 minutes. Preheat the oven to
  180°C (160°C fan oven) mark 4.

4 Bake the pudding(s) in the oven
  for 30–40 minutes. Dust with icing
  sugar to serve.

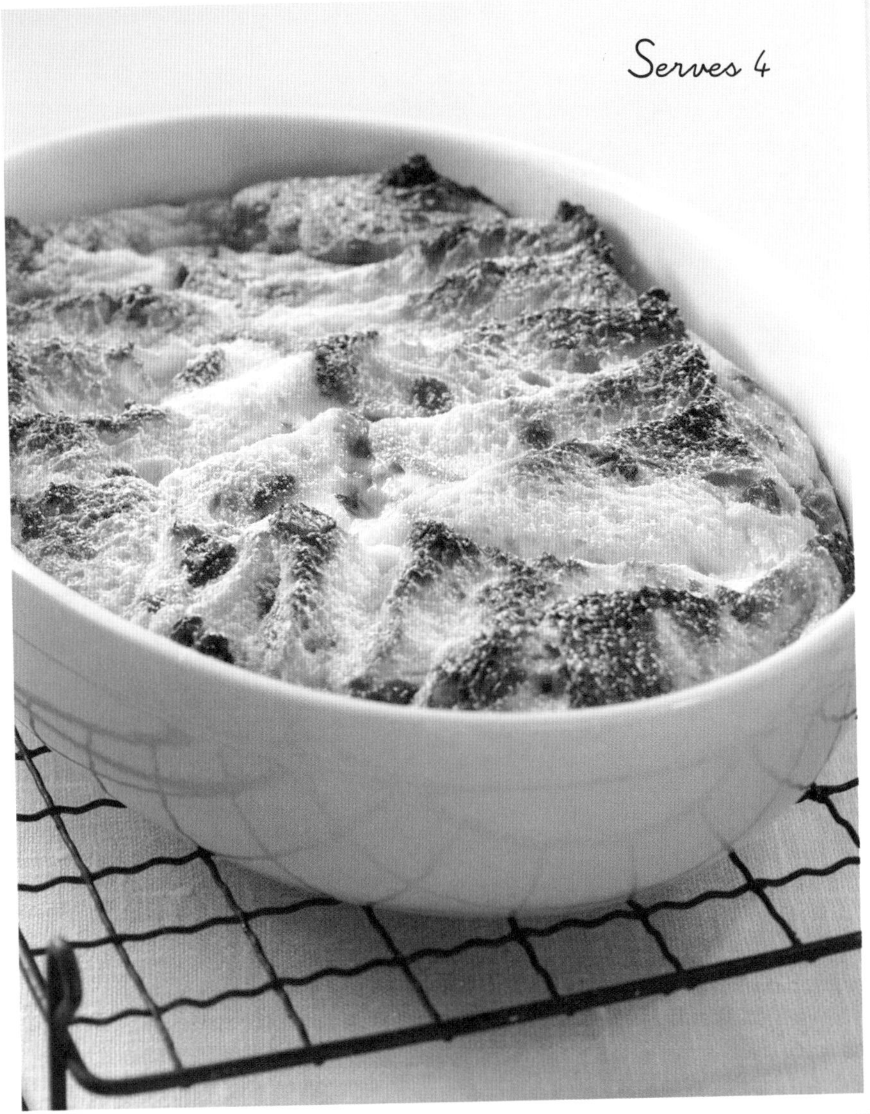
Serves 4

Five-minute Microwave Chocolate Pudding

Hands-on time: about 3 minutes
Cook time: about 1 minute

2½ tbsp cocoa powder
2 tbsp golden syrup
6 tbsp self-raising flour
2½ tbsp caster sugar
1 medium egg
1½ tbsp mild oil
1½ tbsp milk
40g (1½oz) white chocolate,
  finely chopped

1 Divide 1 tbsp of the cocoa powder
  equally between two standard mugs.
  Add 1 tbsp golden syrup to each
  and mix to a paste. Put the flour,
  sugar and remaining 1½ tbsp cocoa
  powder into a medium bowl.

2 Crack in the egg, add the oil and
  milk and mix well, then stir in
  the chocolate.

3 Divide the mixture equally and
  tidily between the mugs, then cook
  on full power in a 800W microwave
  oven for 1 minute 10 seconds.
  Carefully turn out onto a plate
  and serve.

Blondies

Hands-on time: 15 minutes
Cooking time: about 30 minutes, plus cooling

150g (5oz) unsalted butter, chopped,
   plus extra to grease
200g (7oz) white chocolate, chopped
200g (7oz) caster sugar
2 tsp vanilla extract
3 medium eggs
200g (7oz) plain flour
1 tsp baking powder
75g (3oz) white chocolate chips (or use
   finely chopped white chocolate)

1 Preheat the oven to 180°C (160°C fan oven) mark 4. Lightly grease a 20.5cm (8in) square tin and line with baking parchment.

2 Melt the butter and white chocolate in a heatproof bowl set over a pan of barely simmering water (make sure the base of the bowl doesn't touch the water). Lift the bowl off the pan and leave to cool slightly.

3 Beat in the sugar, vanilla extract and eggs until combined. Sift over the flour and baking powder, then fold through most of the chocolate chips.

4 Scrape into the tin, level and scatter over the remaining chocolate chips. Bake for 20–25 minutes until just firm. Leave to cool in the tin, before cutting into squares. Keep wrapped in foil or in an airtight container at room temperature for up to four days.

Cuts into 16 squares

Take 5 Easy Steps to Muesli Bars

Some of the simplest biscuits to make are traybakes, which are cooked in one piece and then cut into bars. The mixtures often contain fruit, nuts and sometimes oats.

To make 12 bars, you will need: 175g (6oz) unsalted butter, cut into pieces, 150g (5oz) light muscovado sugar, 2 tbsp golden syrup, 375g (13oz) porridge oats, 100g (3½oz) ready-to-eat dried papaya, roughly chopped, 50g (2oz) sultanas, 50g (2oz) pecan nuts, roughly chopped, 25g (1oz) pinenuts, 25g (1oz) pumpkin seeds, 1 tbsp plain flour, 1 tsp ground cinnamon.

1 Preheat the oven to 180°C (160°C fan oven) mark 4. Melt the butter, sugar and golden syrup together in a heavy-based pan over a low heat.

2 Meanwhile, put the oats, dried fruit, nuts, seeds, flour and cinnamon into a large bowl

and stir to mix. Pour in the melted mixture and mix together until combined.

3 Spoon the mixture into a 30.5 × 20.5cm (12 × 8in) non-stick baking tin and press down into the corners.

4 Bake for 25–30 minutes until golden. Press the mixture down again if necessary, then use a palette knife to mark into 12 bars.

5 Leave to cool completely. Use a palette knife to lift the bars out of the tin and store in an airtight container.

FREEZE AHEAD
Store individually wrapped muesli bars in the freezer. Remove and thaw for a couple of hours for the perfect mid-morning snack.

Munchy Bars

125g (4oz) butter, roughly chopped

3 × 100g bars plain chocolate, broken into pieces

4 heaped tbsp golden syrup

10 digestive biscuits, broken into smallish chunks

3 mugfuls of Rice Krispies or Coco Pops

2 handfuls of raisins or sultanas

1 Put the butter, chocolate and golden syrup into a large saucepan. Gently heat, stirring constantly, until the mixture is melted, smooth and shiny.

2 Take off the heat and stir in the digestive biscuits, Rice Krispies or Coco Pops and raisins or sultanas.

3 Use baking parchment or clingfilm to line the inside of a small-medium roasting tin or serving dish. Spoon in the chocolate mixture and level the surface. Chill in the fridge to set, cut into bars and eat within two weeks.

Serves 6

220 cal ♥ 7g protein
9g fat (0.6g sat) ♥ 4g fibre
27g carb ♥ 0g salt

10

193 cal ♥ 9g protein
8g fat (1g sat) ♥ 2g fibre
22g carb ♥ 0.4g salt

12

303 cal ♥ 11g protein
6g fat (1g sat) ♥ 6g fibre
48g carb ♥ 0.2g salt

14

220 cal ♥ 9g protein
5g fat (1g sat) ♥ 4g fibre
33g carb ♥ 0.6g salt

18

550 cal ♥ 43g protein
33g fat (11g sat) ♥ 2g fibre
15g carb ♥ 2.7g salt

32

(without pesto and ciabatta)
285 cal ♥ 12g protein
7g fat (1g sat) ♥ 10g fibre
39g carb ♥ 0.1g salt

38

499 cal ♥ 32g protein
13g fat (4g sat) ♥ 7g fibre
60g carb ♥ 0.4g salt

40

340 cal ♥ 3g protein
26g fat (6g sat) ♥ 2g fibre
22g carb ♥ 0.6g salt

50

315 cal ♥ 9g protein
4g fat (0.7g sat) ♥ 8g fibre
53g carb ♥ 0.9g salt

52

391 cal ♥ 14g protein
6g fat (0.8g sat) ♥ 6g fibre
68g carb ♥ 0.9g salt

60

833 cal ♥ 39g protein
45g fat (21g sat) ♥ 6g fibre
60g carb ♥ 1.5g salt

70

589 cal ♥ 34g protein
21g fat (12g sat) ♥ 5g fibre
63g carb ♥ 1.6g salt

72

552 cal ♥ 53g protein
22g fat (6g sat) ♥ 3g fibre
34g carb ♥ 0.5g salt

78

(per serving for 6)
413 cal ♥ 34g protein
28g fat (7g sat) ♥ 2g fibre
6g carb ♥ 0.4g salt

80

730 cal ♥ 27g protein
32g fat (13g sat) ♥ 3g fibre
84g carb ♥ 4g salt

20

468 cal ♥ 21g protein
24g fat (5g sat) ♥ 5g fibre
40g carb ♥ 1g salt

26

128 cal ♥ 7g protein
7g fat (1g sat) ♥ 3g fibre
9g carb ♥ 0.3g salt

28

330 cal ♥ 20g protein
16g fat (6g sat) ♥ 2g fibre
26g carb ♥ 1.9g salt

30

332 cal ♥ 14g protein
10g fat (6g sat) ♥ 8g fibre
42g carb ♥ 1.6g salt

42

497 cal ♥ 27g protein
18g fat (5g sat) ♥ 6g fibre
55g carb ♥ 2g salt

44

268 cal ♥ 12g protein
14g fat (9g sat) ♥ 1g fibre
23g carb ♥ 1.2g salt

46

344 cal ♥ 23g protein
10g fat (2g sat) ♥ 11g fibre
35g carb ♥ 0.3g salt

48

617 cal ♥ 33g protein
26g fat (10g sat) ♥ 3g fibre
62g carb ♥ 2.1g salt

62

724 cal ♥ 44g protein
31g fat (12g sat) ♥ 7g fibre
64g carb ♥ 1.1g salt

64

296 cal ♥ 19g protein
20g fat (7g sat) ♥ 3g fibre
6g carb ♥ 0.7g salt

66

425 cal ♥ 20g protein
11g fat (4g sat) ♥ 5g fibre
58g carb ♥ 1.2g salt

68

669 cal ♥ 34g protein
50g fat (21g sat) ♥ 2g fibre
20g carb ♥ 0.4g salt

82

590 cal ♥ 33g protein
31g fat (14g sat) ♥ 6g fibre
42g carb ♥ 0.6g salt

84

507 cal ♥ 18g protein
34g fat (10g sat) ♥ 3g fibre
31g carb ♥ 2.3g salt

86

304 cal ♥ 22g protein
12g fat (3g sat) ♥ 5g fibre
24g carb ♥ 0.4g salt

88

418 cal ♥ 30g protein
22g fat (8g sat) ♥ 8g fibre
21g carb ♥ 1.5g salt

90

598 cal ♥ 48g protein
15g fat (5g sat) ♥ 4g fibre
66g carb ♥ 1.1g salt

92

290 cal ♥ 19g protein
8g fat (0.7g sat) ♥ 15g fibre
27g carb ♥ 1.4g salt

94

361 cal ♥ 34g protein
19g fat (9g sat) ♥ 2g fibre
13g carb ♥ 1g salt

100

574 cal ♥ 19g protein
18g fat (6g sat) ♥ 5g fibre
82g carb ♥ 2.7g salt

110

417 cal ♥ 22g protein
16g fat (7g sat) ♥ 0.3g fibre
47g carb ♥ 2g salt

112

574 cal ♥ 39g protein
13g fat (2g sat) ♥ 13g fibre
70g carb ♥ 0.8g salt

114

271 cal ♥ 22g protein
13g fat (3g sat) ♥ 4g fibre
16g carb ♥ 0.9g salt

116

(before adding pesto)
411 cal ♥ 18g protein
7g fat (1g sat) ♥ 3g fibre
68g carb ♥ 2.1g salt

134

807 cal ♥ 24g protein
50g fat (28g sat) ♥ 6g fibre
62g carb ♥ 2.2g salt

136

498 cal ♥ 14g protein
30g fat (10g sat) ♥ 7g fibre
39g carb ♥ 3.1g salt

138

584 cal ♥ 36g protein
34g fat (13g sat) ♥ 9g fibre
31g carb ♥ 1.8g salt

140

(without liqueur)
156 cal ♥ 6g protein
4g fat (2g sat) ♥ 1g fibre
24g carb ♥ 0.2g salt

152

317 cal ♥ 6g protein
18g fat (12g sat) ♥ 0g fibre
32g carb ♥ 0.1g salt

154

206 cal ♥ 5g protein
7g fat (0.7g sat) ♥ 3g fibre
29g carb ♥ 0.1g salt

156

546 cal ♥ 8g protein
21g fat (9g sat) ♥ 7g fibre
77g carb ♥ 0.3g salt

158

451 cal ♥ 28g protein
16g fat (6g sat) ♥ 5g fibre
48g carb ♥ 1.1g salt

102

627 cal ♥ 47g protein
36g fat (13g sat) ♥ 3g fibre
27g carb ♥ 3.5g salt

104

553 cal ♥ 22g protein
17g fat (4g sat) ♥ 12g fibre
73g carb ♥ 2.1g salt

106

(without guacamole)
371 cal ♥ 13g protein
8g fat (0.8g sat) ♥ 13g fibre
54g carb ♥ 1.8g salt

108

157 cal ♥ 4g protein
5g fat (1g sat) ♥ 1g fibre
22g carb ♥ 0.5g salt

18

563 cal ♥ 50g protein
39g fat (10g sat) ♥ 0g fibre
0g carb ♥ 0.5g salt

128

284 cal ♥ 34g protein
4g fat (0.5g sat) ♥ 2g fibre
27g carb ♥ 1.1g salt

130

283 cal ♥ 38g protein
10g fat (3g sat) ♥ 2g fibre
9g carb ♥ 2.1g salt

132

199 cal ♥ 9g protein
14g fat (6g sat) ♥ 2g fibre
8g carb ♥ 1.2g salt

42

179 cal ♥ 6g protein
5g fat (0.7g sat) ♥ 7g fibre
23g carb ♥ 0.4g salt

144

360 cal ♥ 13g protein
25g fat (11g sat) ♥ 5g fibre
19g carb ♥ 1.5g salt

146

553 cal ♥ 3g protein
43g fat (27g sat) ♥ 1g fibre
38g carb ♥ 0.2g salt

150

547 cal ♥ 12g protein
21g fat (7g sat) ♥ 4g fibre
76g carb ♥ 0.6g salt

160

516 cal ♥ 10g protein
19g fat (6g sat) ♥ 2g fibre
77g carb ♥ 0.8g salt

162

270 cal ♥ 4g protein
14g fat (8g sat) ♥ 0.5g fibre
31g carb ♥ 0.3g salt

164

680 cal ♥ 6g protein
36g fat (22g sat) ♥ 2g fibre
81g carb ♥ 1.1g salt

168

Index

BAKE ME A CAKE
There's always time for cake

EASY PEASY MEALS
Easy meals for every day

LET'S DO BRUNCH
Mouth-watering meals to start your day

CHEAP EATS
Budget-busting ideas that won't break the ba...

WONDERFUL ONE-POTS
Easy peasy recipes made in just one pot

Available online and from all good bookshops

SUPER SOUPS
Sumptuous soups for every day

SKINNY SUPPERS
Delicious, nutritious recipes under 300 calories

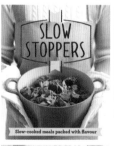

SLOW STOPPERS
Slow-cooked meals packed with flavour

GREAT VEG
Inspired ideas for delicious veggie meals

AL FRESCO EATS
Easy grills, barbecues and picnics

ROAST IT
There's nothing better than a delicious roast

FLASH IN THE PAN
Spice up your noodles and stir-fries

GLUTEN-FREE AND EASY
Oh-so-good-for-you recipes that taste great

LOW FAT LOW CAL
Nice recipes don't need to be naughty

PICTURE CREDITS
Photographers:
Neil Barclay (pages 51, 65); Martin
Brigdale (page 119); Steve Baxter
(pages 63, 73, 7L, 87, 96, 97R, 111,
115, 117, 163); Nicki Dowey (pages
7R, 11, 13, 15, 39, 47, 49, 61, 75R, 81,
83, 85, 91, 105, 113, 143, 147, 157);
Mike English (page 165); Will Heap
(pages 7L, 19); Gareth Morgans
(pages 21, 27, 29, 31, 34, 35R, 41, 45,
89, 97L, 101, 103, 107, 109, 133, 145);
Myles New (pages 33, 43, 123R,
139, 141, 155); Craig Robertson
(pages 16, 17, 22, 23, 24, 25, 35L,
53, 56, 149L, 153, 159, 161, 166, 167);
Maja Smend (page 93); Lucinda
Symons (pages 6, 27, 37, 58, 95);
John Whitaker (pages 54, 55L, 55R,
67, 69, 71, 122, 123L, 131, 135, 137,
148, 149R, 151, 169); Kate Whitaker
(pages 74, 79, 129); Rachel Whiting
(front cover).

Home Economists:
Meike Beck, Anna Burges-
Lumsden, Monaz Dumasia, Joanna
Farrow, Emma Jane Frost, Teresa
Goldfinch, Alice Hart, Zoë Horne,
Jenny Iggleden, Lucy McKelvie,
Jennie Milsom, Kim Morphew, Aya
Nishimura, Katie Rogers, Bridget
Sargeson, Stella Sargeson, Sarah
Tildesley, Kate Trend, Charlotte
Watson, Jennifer White and Mari
Mereid Williams.

Stylists:
Susannah Blake, Tamzin
Ferdinando, Lisa Harrison,
Cynthia Inions, Rachel Jukes,
Penny Markham, Wei Tang, Sarah
Tildesley, Helen Trent, Fanny Ward,
Polly Webb-Wilson and
Mari Mereid Williams.